At Issue

| Concealed Weapons

Other Books in the At Issue Series:

At Issue

| Concealed Weapons

Kacy Lovelace, Book Editor

GREENHAVEN PRESS
A part of Gale, Cengage Learning

GALE
CENGAGE Learning™

Detroit • New York • San Francisco • New Haven, Conn • Waterville, Maine • London

GALE
CENGAGE Learning

Christine Nasso, *Publisher*
Elizabeth Des Chenes, *Managing Editor*

© 2011 Greenhaven Press, a part of Gale, Cengage Learning.

Gale and Greenhaven Press are registered trademarks used herein under license.

For more information, contact:
Greenhaven Press
27500 Drake Rd.
Farmington Hills, MI 48331-3535
Or you can visit our Internet site at gale.cengage.com

For product information and technology assistance, contact us at

Gale Customer Support, 1-800-877-4253
For permission to use material from this text or product, submit all requests online at www.cengage.com/permissions.

Further permissions questions can be e-mailed to permissionrequest@cengage.com.

Articles in Greenhaven Press anthologies are often edited for length to meet page require-ments. In addition, original titles of these works are changed to clearly present the main thesis and to explicitly indicate the author's opinion. Every effort is made to ensure that Greenhaven Press accurately reflects the original intent of the authors. Every effort has been made to trace the owners of copyrighted material.

Cover image copyright © Images.com/Corbis.

LIBRARY OF CONGRESS CATALOGING-IN-PUBLICATION DATA

Concealed weapons / Kacy Lovelace, book editor.
    p. cm. -- (At issue)
    Includes bibliographical references and index.
    ISBN 978-0-7377-5147-5 (hardcover) -- ISBN 978-0-7377-5148-2 (pbk.)
    1. Firearms--Law and legislation--United States. 2. Gun control--United States. I. Lovelace, Kacy. II. Title. III. Series.
    KF3941.C66 2011
    344.730533--dc22
                                           2010042116

Printed in the United States of America
2 3 4 5 6 7 15 14 13 12 11

Contents

Introduction

On July 22, 2009, the United States Senate narrowly defeated S.1618, the Senate Bill Respecting States' Rights and Concealed Carry Reciprocity Act, which was proposed by the Senate Republican Policy Committee chairman and Republican Senator from South Dakota, John Thune. Also referred to as the Thune Amendment, S.1618 was attached to the larger military appropriations bill, Defense Authorization Bill (S. 1390), and provided for the federal reciprocity of concealed carry firearms. Federal reciprocity already exists in the United States for such documents as marriage licenses and driver's licenses; this allows Americans to travel between states without fear that the documents issued by another state will not be recognized. Supporters of federal reciprocity for concealed weapons seek this same recognition between states for permit holders.

Thune contends that federal reciprocity for concealed weapons would decrease crime rates across the country, citing the legality of the carrying of concealed weapons and the safety of his constituents in his home state of South Dakota as the reasoning behind this proposed bill. "South Dakota is one of many states with reasonable measures in place allowing citizens to protect themselves with concealed weapons," Thune says in a July 20, 2009 press release. He continues, "Law-abiding South Dakotans should be able to exercise the right to bear arms in states with similar regulations on concealed firearms. My legislation enables citizens to protect themselves while respecting individual state firearms laws." Thune's bill had thirteen co-sponsors including Republican Senator Orrin Hatch from Utah and Democratic Senator from Arkansas, Mark Begich.

Another of the amendment's co-sponsors, Louisiana Republican Senator David Vitter, explained his support of the amendment in a February 5, 2009 press release: "This bill simply clarifies the rights of gun owners and affords citizens a right that they are already entitled to under US law. By elevating concealed handgun permits to the same status as driver's licenses, we can ensure that an individual possessing a legal permit to carry a concealed weapon from his or her home state is afforded the same privilege in another state that already has concealed carry laws."

Thune's proposed bill, however, was not without opponents. Mayors Against Illegal Guns, a national coalition of over 500 mayors from both small and large US cities who fight to keep criminals from obtaining guns illegally, numbered among those groups trying to stop Thune's bill from passing. In their July 21, 2009 press release in *USA Today*, Mayors Against Illegal Guns called for the defeat of the bill by the United States Senate: "The Thune Amendment requires states to honor concealed weapon carry permits from other states, even if the individual carrying the weapon would otherwise be ineligible to do so. The Mayors Against Illegal Guns coalition has long believed that the issue of concealed carry regulation is one best left to cities and states. The policies that legislators and law enforcement officials adopt in rural areas may not be best for urban areas—and vice-versa. This legislation would mean that the state with the most lax conceal-carry requirements would effectively set the policy for the entire nation."

New York City Mayor and coalition co-chair Michael R. Bloomberg continues: "Under current law in most states, if you have certain misdemeanor convictions, are an alcohol abuser, or haven't completed a gun safety training program, you cannot carry a concealed weapon. This bill would effectively erase those rules. We can't destroy the common sense safeguards states across the country have put in place. The Senate must stop this dangerous measure." Senator Charles Schumer told *Fox News*, "If you walk down the street in New

York . . . you can have the solace of knowing that if someone has a gun on them they've gone through a rigorous police background check. After this bill, you can have no such comfort."

Mayor Bloomberg and Senator Schumer are not the only ones concerned about the effects of the passage of S. 1618 or similar bills for New York State, which is well known for its stringent concealed weapons laws. Currently, New York concealed carry permits are honored in 15 other states. However, New York does not honor permits from any other states. On July 22, 2009, the day of the bill's defeat, former New York County district attorney, Robert M. Morgenthau, wrote in the *Wall Street Journal*: "In New York, the state imposes careful restrictions on who may carry concealed firearms. With the Thune amendment, New York and other states would be obliged to recognize licenses from jurisdictions that choose to issue them practically for the asking. For example, in Ohio and Missouri, virtually any resident without a criminal record or prior hospitalizations for mental illness can carry a gun. Under the Thune amendment, that Midwesterner could legally carry the gun straight into New York, despite New York's more stringent rules." Morgenthau also maintains that Thune's amendment would allow those who had been denied permits in New York to seek permits in states that issue them to non-residents allowing them to bring their weapons into New York.

A July 20, 2009 *New York Times* editorial claimed that such legislation would make the work of the police much more difficult: "Passage of the amendment would make it much harder for law enforcement to distinguish between legal and illegal possession of a firearm. It would be a boon for illegal gun traffickers, making it easier to transport weapons across state lines without being caught." The Thune Amendment constitutes just one element of the concealed carry debate in the United States. In *At Issue: Concealed Weapons*, authors provide a variety of perspectives in their exploration of the myriad of issues concerning concealed weapons. These issues include the safety risks or benefits that concealed weapons provide to the public and permit holders alike, the protection and violation of individual rights in the concealed carry debate, and both the dangers and positive results of allowing concealed weapons in national parks and on college campuses.

1

The Evolution of Concealed Carry Laws: An Overview

Richard S. Grossman and Stephen A. Lee

Richard S. Grossman is Professor and Chairman of the Department of Economics at Wesleyan University, and a Visiting Scholar at the Institute for Quantitative Social Science at Harvard University. Stephen A. Lee is a New Hampshire State Trooper.

State concealed weapons laws fall into two categories: "shall issue," in which the state must issue a permit to anyone meeting all requirements, and "may issue," in which law enforcement may deny applicants at their own discretion and generally require applicants to show necessary cause for carrying a concealed weapon. From 1960 to 2003, the number of "shall issue" states increased from two states to thirty-four states. Crime rates, the policies of neighboring states, and the urbanity of the state were all determining factors in this massive evolution to predominately "shall-issue" legislation.

Gun control has long been a contentious issue for policy makers. Increasingly, academics have weighed in on the consequences of various types of gun control laws. The growth of more extensive data sets and the development of sophisticated econometric tools with which to analyze them has led to an explosion in the growth of the academic literature on gun control. In important—and controversial—work, Bronars and Lott (1998), Lott and Mustard (1997), and Lott (1998, 2000,

2003) analyzed an unprecedented volume of statistical data on gun control and crime statistics. They found that more liberal gun control laws (i.e., those that make it easier for law-abiding citizens to obtain firearms) led to a reduction in the incidence of violent crime. [Additional studies, including] Black and Nagin (1998), Ludwig (1998), and Ayres and Donahue (2003), among others, have critiqued both the methodology and the conclusions of Lott et al.'s findings; Bartley and Cohen (1998), Helland and Tabarrok (2004), Plassmann and Whitely (2003), among others, support Lott et al.'s results.

The goal of this paper is not to reassess the debate over the consequences of various gun control regimes, but instead to explain the timing and pattern of the adoption of different gun control laws across U.S. states during the past 40 [years]. There are a wide variety of such laws. These include restrictions on categories of people who are allowed to buy firearms (e.g., felons, misdemeanor offenders, juvenile offenders, aliens, minors, those subject to a restraining order, the mentally ill), limitations on types of firearms allowed (e.g., handguns, assault weapons, machine guns), and regulations on sales (e.g., purchases per month, licensing of dealers, restrictions on gun show and private sales, waiting periods, background checks).

Opponents argue that more widespread gun ownership leads to an increase in the homicide rate.

Types of Concealed Weapons Laws

Rather than examine all of these restrictions, we instead focus on states' concealed-carry handgun laws. These laws typically fall into one of two categories. "Shall issue" laws require that the issuing authority (e.g., a police chief or other public safety official) in a jurisdiction (typically a municipality or county) "shall issue" gun permits to qualified applicants. In other words, the authorities do not have discretion to decide whether or not an applicant has a good reason for needing a permit and will normally be required to issue a permit unless there is some disqualifying factor (e.g., the applicant is a convicted felon). In contrast, "may issue" laws allow the issuing authority to require applicants to state a reason for needing to carry a concealed weapon (e.g., having a dangerous profession, having been stalked in the past) and to issue—or not issue—a gun permit at the discretion of the issuing authority. "May issue," then, is a far more restrictive gun control regime that allows the issuing authority some—and in many cases, considerable—latitude to deny an application.

Concealed Weapons Laws Are the Central Issue of the Gun-Rights Debate

We focus on concealed-carry laws for several reasons. First, concealed-carry laws are at the very center of the current handgun debate. Those in favor of less restrictive concealed-carry laws tout the deterrent effect of concealed handguns, including encouraging crime and criminals to migrate to neighboring jurisdictions with more restrictive concealed-carry rules. Opponents argue that more widespread gun ownership leads to an increase in the homicide rate and claim that an overabundance of concealed handguns encourages spontaneous violence. Second, the shift from "may issue" to "shall issue" has been dramatic in recent years: in 1960, there were just two "shall issue" states; by 1990, the number had risen to 14; and by 2003, the number stood at 34. Finally, relative to other gun control laws, the "shall issue" versus "may issue" distinction is fairly easy to categorize. Although 49 states have laws against felons owning handguns, there are substantial differences across states as to what constitutes a felony and what category of felon is to be denied a handgun permit, making a simple categorization difficult. In contrast, analyzing the decision to enact "shall issue" or "may issue" laws is more straightforward.

Understanding the forces underlying the "shall issue" versus "may issue" decision is important for several reasons. First, gun control is still an important and hotly debated issue. By better understanding the motivations for the timing and adoption of gun control laws, we can explain the geographic and temporal pattern of the spread of gun control legislation across the country. If our analysis of the adoption of "shall issue" laws is successful, it may be extended to other aspects of gun control. Second, as noted above, although a great deal of ink has been spilled trying to determine the consequences of various gun laws, virtually none has been devoted to explaining their genesis. Thus, this project fills a gap in the literature and may help to alleviate problems of simultaneity inherent in work on gun control. Finally, since there is no generally accepted explanation for the peculiar patchwork pattern of gun laws in the United States, explaining the pattern and timing of the adoption of this relatively straightforward measure may pave the way for studies of the adoption of other enactments, including those unrelated to gun control, that are of interest to economists, political scientists, and policy makers.

In most of the United States, laws regulating the concealed carrying of a handgun are of a relatively recent vintage.

We find strong evidence that more urban states are less likely to shift to "shall issue" than rural states. Despite the statistical robustness of this finding, the effect is quantitatively small. We also find evidence that the switch is influenced by the decisions taken by neighboring states. Although this result is less robust than that on urbanization, the quantitative effect is much larger. We also find evidence to suggest that changes in a state's concealed-carry laws are related to the change in, but not the level of, the crime rate.

The History of Concealed Weapons Laws

In most of the United States, laws regulating the concealed carrying of a handgun are of a relatively recent vintage. Although some states did address the issue of concealed-carry prior to the Civil War, they typically did so by banning the practice altogether, including among on-duty law enforcement personnel. During the 1920s and 1930s, many states adopted laws that prohibited unlicensed concealed carrying. In time, most states adopted provisions allowing a local authority to issue concealed handgun permits. According to Cramer and Kopel, ". . . such statutes were broadly discretionary; while the law might specify certain minimum standards for obtaining a permit, the decision whether a permit should be issued was not regulated by express statutory standards." Laws granting the authorities discretion over the issue of concealed carry permits, "may issue" laws, predominated in the early post-World War II period: by 1960, only two states, Vermont and New Hampshire, had "shall issue" laws. During the 1960s, just two states enacted "shall issue" laws: Washington (1961) and Connecticut (1969). By 1990, another 10 states had enacted "shall issue" laws: Indiana (1980), Maine, North Dakota (1985), South Dakota (1986), Florida (1987), Georgia, Oregon, Pennsylvania, West Virginia (1989), and Idaho (1990). Another 16 states followed suit in the 1990s, and 5 more during the period 2000–2003.

At first glance, there is no obvious explanation for the timing or geographic pattern of the adoption of "shall issue" laws. Early adopters include both rural (New Hampshire and Vermont) and less rural (Connecticut) New England states. Following Connecticut's adoption in 1969, a full decade passed before any more states adopted "shall issue" laws. By 1990, "shall issue" had spread to the Midwest, plains, and southern states. After 1990, the adoption of "shall issue" laws spread rapidly to all sections of the country. By 2003, only 16 states, concentrated primarily in the northeast, remained "may issue."

Although many of these "may issue" states are heavily urban (California, Hawaii, Illinois, Massachusetts, New Jersey, New York, and Rhode Island), a number of "may issue" states are much less so (Alabama, Kansas, Nebraska, Iowa, and New Mexico). We consider urbanization and other potential explanations in the following section.

Those who oppose strict control argue that guns in possession of law-abiding citizens reduce the level of crime.

Why would a "may issue" state enact a "shall issue" law? That is, why would states wish to make it easier for citizens to obtain a concealed carry permit? Through our reading of the academic literature, both in favor and opposed to concealed-carry, as well as debates among policy makers and the public, we have discerned several motivating factors.

Crime Rates Affect the Evolution of Concealed Weapons Laws

Crime ranks high on the list of motivations, both for those who argue for and those who argue against stricter gun control laws. Proponents of gun control argue that reducing the number of guns in circulation reduces the level of handgun violence; those who oppose strict control argue that guns in possession of law-abiding citizens reduce the level of crime by deterring potential criminals and allow ordinary citizens to protect themselves. At a rally in Salt Lake City prior to the adoption of Utah's "shall issue" law, proponents argued that a rising crime rate made it important for law-abiding citizens to be able to purchase guns. Lott (2000) and Lott and Mustard (1997) emphasize this view.

The Laws of Surrounding States Affect Concealed Weapons Laws

Another factor cited in support of "shall issue" legislation is a desire to be in step with neighboring jurisdictions. Bronars and Lott (1998) argue that failure to adopt "shall issue" laws may lead to spillover effects, with crime spreading to jurisdictions with more restrictive gun control laws. Politicians have likewise argued that the adoption of "shall issue" laws in surrounding states should encourage passage at home, although *why* a state might want to be in step with its neighbors is frequently left unexplained. For example, according to a sponsor of the Ohio "shall issue" law: "This bill is about putting Ohio in step with the 43 other states that have this law. . . . We are trying to stay in step with the states that are our neighbors." It may be that politicians find "keeping in step with neighboring jurisdictions" a politically less controversial justification than relying on a "more guns, less crime" argument.

Urban Counties Issue More Concealed Weapons Permits

As noted above, states remaining "may issue" appear to be concentrated among the more urbanized states. Might states with a higher proportion of urban dwellers decide that concealed carry ought to be restricted? Conversely, might states with a high proportion of rural dwellers, perhaps more accustomed to gun ownership and hunting, be more comfortable with widespread concealed carry? There has been some evidence of this both in the public debate and in policy. In Virginia. for example, debate over a "shall issue" law in 1995 illustrated the differences between rural and urban judges in issuing concealed carry permits. During 1993–1994, judges in rural Henry County issued 655 permits; during the same period, judges in Washington, DC-area Arlington County issued only 23 permits, while those in neighboring Fairfax County issued just 1.

The Motivations Behind Concealed Weapons Laws

Political factors may also influence the decision to adopt "shall issue" laws. Republicans are widely considered to be more favorable to gun ownership. Consequently, Republican control of state government (i.e., both legislature and governor) may influence the decision to adopt more liberal gun control laws. Lott and Mustard (1997) and Lott (2000) have found that states adopting right to carry laws are relatively Republican with large NRA memberships. . . .

Less urban states are more likely to shift to "shall issue" than their more urban counterparts.

Handgun control, particularly concealed-carry regulation, is among the most hotly debated topics in academic and political circles. Proponents of less stringent gun control argue that guns in the hands of law-abiding citizens can reduce the rate of violent crime; opponents argue that less stringent concealed-carry laws lead to increased levels of crime. In this paper, we take no position on the consequences of concealed-carry laws, but merely attempt to explain the timing and pattern of their adoption.

Our evidence suggests several findings. First, we find strong evidence that less urban states are more likely to shift to "shall issue" than their more urban counterparts, although the effect is quantitatively small. Second, we find evidence—less robust statistically but more substantial—that the decision to enact "shall issue" is influenced by the decisions taken by neighboring states. It is not clear from our research whether this is done merely to avoid being out of step with neighboring jurisdictions or to prevent the spillover effects posited by Bronars and Lott (1998). We have found anecdotal evidence of the former, although this may be because such an argument is less controversial.

We do not find strong evidence that Republican or Democratic control of state government was responsible for the switch to "shall issue," despite anecdotal evidence that suggests that nationally, Republicans are friendlier toward gun ownership than Democratics. It may be that partisan effects are overwhelmed by other influences. Finally, we find no evidence that the level of the crime rate has led to changes in concealed-carry laws. Coefficients on the crime rate, both the total crime rate and the violent crime rate, are not statistically significant. Although the level of the crime rate does not have a statistically significant effect, the change in the crime rate has a positive and statistically significant effect, suggesting that "shall issue" laws are a response to rising crime rates.

2

Laws Permitting Concealed Weapons Ensure Public Safety

Cliff Stearns

Cliff Stearns is a Republican Representative to the United States House of Representatives representing Florida's 6th Congressional District.

Studies have found that those who use concealed weapons to deter a criminal are less likely to suffer injury than those unarmed during an attack. In another study, 40% of convicted felons admitted to being deterred by the possibility of a concealed weapon. Not allowing citizens to protect themselves with a concealed weapon is morally wrong, leading to needless death and a denial of the inherent right to self defense. Additionally, this right should not be limited to the confines of the permit holders' home state, but should allow them to defend themselves while traveling throughout the United States.

The right to bear arms is more than a Constitutional right: every human being has the natural unalienable right to self-defense. [The Roman philosopher] Cicero said 2,000 years ago, "If our lives are endangered by plots or violence or armed robbers or enemies, any and every method of protecting ourselves is morally right."

The U.S. Constitution, the constitutions of 44 states, common law, and the laws of all 50 states recognize the right to use arms in self-defense. Right to carry laws respect the right to self-defense by allowing individuals to carry concealed firearms for their own protection.

Decreasing Crime with Concealed Weapons Laws

So many liberal politicians and self-appointed experts want to keep honest Americans from having access to firearms, even though, since 2003, in states which allow concealed carry, violent crime rates have been lower than anytime since the mid-1970s. The reverse logic of this "knee jerk" reaction is astounding and has lead to an outright assault on our basic Constitutional and natural rights. These misguided policies to keep firearms out of the hands of law-abiding citizens literally mean a death sentence for thousands of Americans.

Look at the facts. According to a study by criminologist Gary Kleck of Florida State University, "[R]obbery and assault victims who used a gun to resist were less likely to be attacked or to suffer an injury than those who used any other methods of self-protection or those who did not resist at all." In approximately 2.5 million instances each year, someone uses a firearm, predominantly a handgun, for self defense in this nation.

In research sponsored by the U.S. Department of Justice, in which almost 2,000 felons were interviewed, 34% of felons said they had been "scared off, shot at, wounded or captured by an armed victim" and 40% of these criminals admitted that they had been deterred from committing a crime out of fear that the potential victim was armed.

Allowing law-abiding people to arm themselves offers more than peace of mind for those individuals—it pays off for everybody through lower crime rates. Statistics from the FBI's Uniformed Crime Report of 2007 show that states with right-to-carry laws have a 30% lower homicide rate, 46% lower robbery, and 12% lower aggravated assault rate and a 22% lower overall violent crime rate than do states without such laws. That is why more and more states have passed right-to-carry laws over the past decade.

Since adopting a concealed carry law Florida's total violent crime rate has dropped 32%.

Florida's Concealed Weapons Model

In 1987, my home state of Florida enacted a "shall issue" law that has become the model for other states. Anti-gun groups, politicians and the news media predicted the new law would lead to vigilante justice and "Wild West" shootouts on every corner.

But since adopting a concealed carry law Florida's total violent crime rate has dropped 32% and its homicide rate has dropped 58%. Floridians, except for criminals, are safer due to this law. And Florida is not alone. Texas' violent crime rate has dropped 20% and homicide rate has dropped 31%, since enactment of its 1996 carry law.

The Moral Case for Concealed Weapons

Another study makes the moral case for expanding and enhancing right-to-carry laws. A report by John Lott, Jr. and David Mustard of the University of Chicago released in 1996 found "that allowing citizens to carry concealed weapons deters violent crimes and it appears to produce no increase in accidental deaths." Further, the Lott-Mustard study noted, "If those states which did not have right-to-carry concealed gun provisions had adopted them in 1992, approximately 1,570 murders; 4,177 rapes; and over 60,000 aggravated assaults would have been avoided yearly."

Think about it. Nearly 8,000 of our fellow citizens have died between 1992 and 1996 because of the irrational fear that law-abiding Americans would abuse their right to self defense.

In fact concealed carry permit holders are more law-abiding than the rest of the public. For example, Florida, which has issued more carry permits than any state has issued 1.36 million permits, but revoked only 165 (0.01%) due to gun crimes by permit-holders.

Laws allowing the concealed carrying of a firearm are on the books in 48 states, in some form. Two-thirds of Americans live in states with right-to-carry laws, their respective state houses and governors recognizing their fundamental right to self-defense. But let me pose a question. Should your natural right to self defense and your Constitutional right to bear arms end when you cross a state line? I think not.

It doesn't make sense to me for Americans to forfeit their safety because they happen to be on vacation or on a business trip.

The Need for National Concealed Weapons Laws

That is why I, along with Representative Rich Boucher (D-Va.) introduced H.R. 197, the National Right-to-Carry Reciprocity Act. Our legislation proposes a federal law that would entitle any person with a valid state-issued concealed carry permit to carry in any other state, as follows: In a state that issues carry permits, its laws would apply. In states that don't issue carry permits, the Federal law providing a "bright-line" standard would permit carrying in places other than police stations; courthouses; public polling places; meetings of state, county, or municipal governing bodies; schools; passenger areas of airports; etc. The bright-light standard in itself is not a license—the individual would still have to possess a valid state permit issued by their state of residence. It doesn't make sense to me for Americans to forfeit their safety because they happen to be on vacation or on a business trip. This legislation would greatly enhance the safety of this nation's ever-increasing mobile society.

As Thomas Jefferson wrote, "No free man shall ever be debarred the use of arms." Our society is a violent society. However, the innocent deserve access to the tools they need to defend themselves. By passing H.R. 197, we can help reduce the carnage wrought by armed criminals. Let's give those who decide to take the responsibility of possessing a concealed carry permit a fighting chance anywhere in America.

3

Gun-Free Zones Increase Instances of Violence

John R. Lott, Jr.

John R. Lott Jr., is a resident scholar at the American Enterprise Institute. Lott has published more than ninety articles in academic journals, including the Journal of Law and Economics *and the* Journal of Legal Studies, *and is a frequent contributor to major newspapers.*

Gun-free zones prevent law-abiding citizens from protecting themselves by taking away the right of a concealed weapons permit holder to carry their weapon in designated areas. Signs designating a gun-free zone only serve to make criminals aware that people within this designated area are unarmed and unprotected. Criminals intent on doing harm are not concerned with the relatively short prison sentences that they will receive for a concealed weapons violation, as they are generally miniscule in comparison to the sentence that they receive for their other crimes. Media bias is detrimental to the cause of liberalizing concealed weapons laws, only showing instances of violence and never showing instances of guns being used in defensive, positive ways, even though research shows that states with liberal concealed weapons laws have lower crime rates, while strict gun-control laws increase instances of homicide.

The last ten days [March 11, 2005–March 21, 2005 saw] three horrific multiple-victim public shootings: the [March 11] Atlanta courthouse attack that left four murdered;

John R. Lott Jr., "Disarming Citizens and Multiple Murders," *National Review*, March 23, 2005. Reproduced by permission.

the [March 14] Wisconsin church shooting, where seven were murdered, and Monday's [March 21] high-school shooting in Minnesota, where nine were murdered. What can be learned from these attacks? Some take the attacks as confirmation that guns should be completely banned from even courthouses, let alone schools and churches.

The threat of using the gun against a criminal can allow one to capture him.

The lessons from the courthouse shooting are likely to be different from the other two attacks in that there were armed sheriff's deputies present. Even if civilian gun possession were banned at the courthouse, the officers still had guns. Not only did they fail to stop the attack, they even facilitated it, because the 200-pound former football linebacker who was facing trial for rape was able to take the gun.

Guns are most useful in stopping criminals at a distance. The threat of using the gun against a criminal can allow one to capture him; or at least can cause the criminal to break off his attack. Police have a much more difficult job than civilians. While civilians can use a gun to maximize the distance between themselves and criminals, police can not be satisfied with simply brandishing a gun and watching the criminal run away. Their job requires physical contact, and when that happens, things can go badly wrong.

My own published research on criminals assaulting police shows that the more likely that an assault will be successful, the more likely criminals will be to make it. The major factor determining success is the relative strengths and sizes of the criminal and officer. In particular, when officer strength and size requirements are reduced because of affirmative action, each one-percent increase in the number of female officers increases the number of assaults on police by 15 to 19 percent. The Atlanta-courthouse shooting simply arose from such a case.

Gun-Free Zones Attract Crime

There is a broader lesson to learn from these attacks. All three attacks took place in areas where gun possession by those who did the attack as well as civilians generally was already banned—so-called "gun-free safe zones." Suppose you or your family are being stalked by a criminal who intends on harming you. Would you feel safer putting a sign in front of your home saying "This Home is a Gun-Free Zone"?

It is pretty obvious why we don't put these signs up. As with many other gun laws, law-abiding citizens, not would-be criminals, would obey the sign. Instead of creating a safe zone for victims, it leaves victims defenseless and creates a safe zone for those intent on causing harm.

A three-year prison term for violating a gun-free zone represents a real penalty for a law-abiding citizen. Adding three years to a criminal's sentence when he is probably already going to face multiple death penalties or life sentences for a murderous rampage is probably not going to be the penalty that stops the criminal from committing his crime.

Instead of creating a safe zone for victims, [gun-free zones] leave victims defenseless.

States with Liberal Concealed Weapons Laws Have Lower Crime Rates

Many Americans have learned this lesson the hard way. In 1985, just eight states had the most liberal right-to-carry laws—laws that automatically grant permits once applicants pass a criminal background check, pay their fees and, when required, complete a training class. Today the total is 37 states. Bill Landes and I have examined all the multiple-victim public shootings with two or more victims in the United States from 1977 to 1999 and found that when states passed right-to-carry laws, these attacks fell by 60 percent. Deaths and injuries from multiple-victim public shootings fell on average by 78 percent.

No other gun-control law had any beneficial effect. Indeed, right-to-carry laws were the only policy that consistently reduced these attacks.

To the extent attacks still occurred in right-to-carry states, they overwhelmingly happened in the special places within those states where concealed handguns were banned. The impact of right-to-carry laws on multiple-victim public shootings is much larger than on other crimes, for a simple reason. Increasing the probability that someone will be able to protect themselves, increases deterrence. Even when any single person might have a small probability of having a concealed handgun, the probability that at least someone will is very high.

Restrictions Placed on Concealed Weapons

Unfortunately, the restrictive concealed-handgun law now in effect in Minnesota bans concealed handguns around schools and Wisconsin is one of four states that completely ban concealed handguns, let alone not allowing them in churches. (There was a guard at the Minnesota school and he was apparently the first person killed, but he was also apparently unarmed.) While permitted concealed handguns by civilians are banned in Georgia courthouses, it is not clear that the benefit is anywhere near as large as other places simply because you usually have armed law enforcement nearby. One possibility is to encourage prosecutors and others to carry concealed guns around courthouses.

These restrictions on guns in schools weren't always in place. Prior to the end of 1995 when the Safe School Zone Act was enacted, virtually all the states that allowed citizens, whether they be teacher or principles or parents, to carry concealed handguns let them carry them on school grounds. Even Minnesota used to allow this.

Some have expressed fears over letting concealed permit holders carry guns on school campuses, but over all the years that permitted guns were allowed on school property there is no evidence that these guns were used improperly or caused any accidents.

Just as the threat of arrest and prison can deter criminals from committing a crime, so can the fact that victims can defend themselves.

The Media Is Biased Against Concealed Weapons

People's reaction to the horrific events displayed on TV such as the Minnesota attack are understandable, but the more than two million times each year that Americans use guns defensively are never discussed—even though this is five times as often as the 450,000 times that guns are used to commit crimes over the last couple of years. Seldom do cases make the news where public shootings are stopped or mothers use guns to prevent their children from being kidnapped. Few would know that a third of the public-school shootings were stopped by citizens with guns before uniformed police could arrive.

In an analysis that I did during 2001 of media coverage of guns, the morning and evening national-news broadcasts on the three main television networks carried almost 200,000 words on contemporaneous gun-crime stories. By comparison, not one segment featured a civilian using a gun to stop a crime. Newspapers are not much better.

Police are extremely important in deterring crime, but they almost always arrive after the crime has been committed. Annual surveys of crime victims in the United States continually show that, when confronted by a criminal, people are safest if they have a gun. Just as the threat of arrest and prison can deter criminals from committing a crime, so can the fact that victims can defend themselves.

Strict Gun-Control Laws Increase Homicide Rates

Gun-control advocates conveniently ignore that the nations with the highest homicide rates have gun bans. Studies, such as one conducted recently by Jeff Miron at Boston University, which examined 44 countries, find that stricter gun-control laws tend to lead to higher homicide rates. Russia, which has banned guns since the Communist revolution, has had murder rates several times higher than that of the United States; even under the Communists, the Soviet Union's rate was much higher.

Good intentions don't necessarily make good laws.

What counts is whether the laws ultimately save lives. Unfortunately, too many gun laws primarily disarm law-abiding citizens, not criminals.

4

Weak Laws Permitting Concealed Weapons Endanger Public Safety

Legal Community Against Violence

Legal Community Against Violence is a public interest law center dedicated to preventing gun violence. Founded by lawyers, LCAV is the country's only organization devoted exclusively to providing legal assistance in support of gun violence prevention.

Over the past two decades, the gun lobby has succeeded in weakening state laws that regulate the carrying of concealed weapons. Thanks to the gun lobby's increasingly vigorous efforts in this area, state legislatures across America have removed law enforcement discretion from the concealed weapon permitting process, significantly expanded the places in which permit holders may carry concealed firearms, and otherwise made permits dangerously easy to acquire. Contrary to the claims of the gun lobby, research shows that permissive concealed carry laws do not decrease crime. In fact, these laws may increase crime. States that choose to permit the carrying of concealed weapons may adopt common sense policies to reduce the risks created by permissive concealed carry laws.

In the summer of 2009, many Americans were shocked to see images of gun-toting protestors at town hall meetings across the country, and even more shocked to learn that this outrageous behavior was perfectly legal. The scary truth is that 32 states allow a person to openly carry a loaded handgun without a permit. But while open carrying has received widespread media attention, there are significant numbers of guns in public that we don't see. Hidden in plain sight, rising numbers of Americans are carrying concealed, loaded handguns in public places.

Thanks to a relentless campaign by the gun lobby, state concealed carry laws (commonly known as "CCW" laws) aren't just bad; they're getting worse. Over the past two decades, state legislatures across America have removed law enforcement discretion from the permitting process, significantly expanded the places in which permit holders may carry concealed firearms, and otherwise made permits dangerously easy to acquire.

Americans want solutions to our nation's gun violence epidemic.

Most Americans Oppose Easing Concealed Carry Permit Requirements

The gun lobby continues to push legislatures to expand carrying, despite the fact that public opinion polls confirm that Americans feel less safe when their fellow citizens carry concealed guns. Americans overwhelmingly do not want concealed carry permits to be easier to acquire, with 73% opposing easing permit requirement, and nine-out-of-ten respondents stating they do not want average citizens to be able to carry guns into places like restaurants, college campuses, sports stadiums, bars, hospitals, or government buildings. In fact, more than 40 percent of Americans support a nationwide ban on the carrying of concealed firearms.

Americans want solutions to our nation's gun violence epidemic—which kills more than 30,000 and injures almost

70,000 each year—and understand that widespread carrying of concealed weapons isn't the answer; it's part of the problem.

In this publication, [Legal Community Against Violence, or LCAV] examines the laws that facilitate the widespread carrying of guns within our midst. As discussed below:

- State concealed carry laws vary widely. In some states, individuals must demonstrate a justifiable need to carry a concealed weapon. The vast majority of states, however, do not require "good cause," and mandate the issuance of a license to anyone who meets minimal requirements.

- Most existing CCW permitting schemes are full of dangerous gaps, allowing too many people to carry weapons in too many public places.

- Contrary to the claims of the gun lobby, research shows that permissive CCW laws do not decrease crime. In fact, these laws may increase crime.

- Federal legislation to require states to recognize out-of-state CCW permits would force states to allow carrying by persons who would not meet the requirements for in-state permits.

- The Second Amendment presents no barrier to strong regulation of concealed weapons.

- States that choose to permit the carrying of concealed weapons may adopt common sense policies to reduce the risks created by permissive CCW laws.

Concealed Weapons Laws Vary Greatly Between States

Whether and to what extent individuals may carry concealed weapons in public are primarily questions of state law. Different states have very different laws, and many states have significantly changed their laws over time. Although laws prohibiting the carrying of concealed weapons date back to the early 1800s, states began to grant law enforcement discretion to issue CCW permits in the first few decades of the 20th century. It was not until the 1990s, however, that, at the behest of the gun lobby, large numbers of state legislatures began to enact laws removing law enforcement discretion from the permitting process and otherwise significantly weakening CCW laws.

Today, thirty-four states are "shall issue" states—meaning law enforcement officials are required to issue a permit to anyone who meets minimal statutory requirements (e.g., that the applicant is over the age of 21, has not been convicted of a felony, and is a United States citizen). Eleven states are "may issue" states, and give discretion to the issuing official to grant or deny a permit application based on various statutory factors, such as whether the applicant has "good cause," i.e., a justifiable need to carry a concealed weapon. Two of those states—Delaware and New Jersey—require court approval of CCW permit applications.

Illinois, Wisconsin, and the District of Columbia prohibit the carrying of concealed weapons, and no permit is required to carry a concealed weapon in Alaska, Arizona, or Vermont.

In every state that issues CCW permits, an applicant may not receive a permit if he or she is prohibited from purchasing firearms due to a disqualifying criminal conviction. In some states, a person will become prohibited after being convicted of a felony or one of a number of misdemeanors, in others, the number of disqualifying misdemeanors is far more limited.

Several studies of CCW permitting systems have identified flawed application processes that have allowed numerous persons prohibited from possessing firearms to receive CCW permits. In Florida, for example, more than 1,400 individuals who had pled guilty or no contest to felonies, 216 individuals with outstanding warrants, 128 people with active domestic violence injunctions against them, and 6 registered sex offenders held CCW permits in the first half of 2006. Unfortunately, Florida is hardly alone in issuing permits to convicted felons: reports have also documented flawed processes in Indiana, Tennessee and Texas.

Eleven states do not require a CCW permit applicant to complete a firearm safety course. Moreover, states that do require applicants to take safety courses rarely articulate the important elements that a course should contain, including education about federal and state firearms laws, demonstration of proper firearm handling and safe storage techniques, instruction in non-violent dispute resolution, and participation in live firing. Even more troubling, a recent Virginia law actually allows applicants to satisfy their required safety instruction through an online program.

State legislatures have recognized that concealed weapons on college campuses . . . are overwhelmingly opposed by the American public.

Gun-Free Zones Protect Public Safety

CCW permits generally entitle permit holders to carry hidden, loaded firearms in any public place except where explicitly prohibited. Most states, unfortunately, do not prohibit carrying at many locations where large numbers of defenseless people congregate, or where interpersonal conflicts are commonplace. The majority of states prohibit concealed weapons on school property and in courthouses and other government buildings. Significantly fewer, however, prohibit concealed weapons in locations where liquor is served, places of worship, sports arenas, public parks, medical facilities, sites where gambling is permitted or polling places. At any of these locations, the accidental or intentional use of a gun could seriously jeopardize public safety.

Although the gun lobby has, since 2007, made more than 30 attempts to expand CCW laws across America to allow carrying on college campuses—arguing that concealed weapons could prevent a tragedy like the Virginia Tech massacre—efforts to bring concealed weapons into classrooms have been unsuccessful. Fortunately, state legislatures have recognized that concealed weapons on college campuses would needlessly place college students at an increased risk for accidental shootings, drug- and alcohol-related violence and suicide, and are overwhelmingly opposed by the American public.

Many state CCW permit holders receive an extra benefit from their permits under federal law: if their permits qualify, they do not need to undergo background checks before purchasing new firearms. Under federal law, a CCW permit holder is exempt from a background check if the permit was issued within the last five years and the permit application included a background check using the National Instant Criminal Background Check System. Without a check with each firearm purchase, however, a firearms dealer is unable to confirm that a buyer has not been convicted of a crime or otherwise become ineligible to possess firearms since the date his or her CCW permit was issued. For this reason, some states do not seek the exemption, and require background checks for firearm purchases by permit holders.

The gun lobby's outrageous claim that guns are used defensively 2.5 million times every year has been widely discredited.

Permissive Concealed Carry Laws Do Not Reduce Crime

Claims that permissive CCW laws lead to decreases in crime—by helping permit holders fight off criminals and sending the message to would-be attackers that any potential victim might be packing heat—are simply not true. No credible statistical evidence exists to show that permissive CCW laws reduce crime. In fact, the evidence suggests that permissive CCW laws may actually increase crime. Important research confirms the common sense conclusion that more guns create more opportunities for injury and death, not fewer.

The gun lobby's outrageous claim that guns are used defensively 2.5 million times every year has been widely discredited. The claim is based on a study that suffers from several fatal methodological flaws, including its reliance on only 66 responses in a telephone survey of 5,000 people, multiplied out to purportedly represent 200 million American adults.

Even when a gun is used in self-defense, which is rare, the research shows that it is no more likely to reduce a person's chance of being injured during a crime than various other forms of protective action. One recent study suggests that carrying a firearm may actually increase a victim's risk of firearm injury during the commission of a crime.

Moreover, studies show that much of what is claimed to be self-defense is actually criminal gun use that creates or exacerbates interpersonal conflicts. In one study, after individuals were asked to provide detailed descriptions of their alleged defensive gun use, a group of criminal court judges anonymously evaluated the responses and concluded that at least half of the uses were probably illegal, including, for example, the conduct of a man who threatened to shoot an unarmed acquaintance who interrupted him while he was watching a movie at home.

Although legislatures continue to enact laws to expand concealed carrying, more research is needed regarding the impact of permissive CCW laws. One comprehensive study strongly supports the contention that more carrying makes society less safe. It found that Texas CCW permit holders were arrested for weapons-related crimes at a rate 81% higher than that of the state's general adult population. Additionally, recent research has identified CCW permit holders who killed at least 43 private citizens and 7 law enforcement officers in incidents that ended in criminal charges or the shooter's suicide between May 2007 and April 2009.

Attempt to Limit State Authority to Regulate Carrying of Concealed Weapons

As part of its never-ending quest to expand the carrying of concealed weapons, the gun lobby has begun to attack state control over CCWs. In 2009, Senator John Thune introduced an amendment to federal legislation that would have required every state that issues CCW permits to recognize all permits issued by other states. "Forced reciprocity" eviscerates every state's right to determine the requirements for carrying a concealed weapon within the state, and threatens the small number of states that have strong permitting schemes, since they would be forced to recognize permit holders who would have not met the requirements for in-state permits. Although Senator Thune's amendment was narrowly defeated in July 2009, new legislation to force reciprocity will likely emerge in the future.

Despite the gun lobby's rhetoric, the Second Amendment presents no barrier to strong regulation of concealed weapons. *In District of Columbia v. Heller*, the Supreme Court held for the first time that the Second Amendment guarantees an individual right to possess a firearm in the home for self-defense. The Court struck down Washington, D.C.'s decades-old ban on handgun possession, and the requirement that firearms in the home be stored unloaded and disassembled or bound by a locking device (which had no exception for self-defense).

The *Heller* Court emphasized, however, that the right protected is "not a right to keep and carry any weapon whatsoever in any manner whatsoever and for whatever purpose." *Heller* also noted that laws prohibiting firearm possession in "sensitive places" (including schools and government buildings) were presumptively valid.

In *McDonald v. Chicago*, the United States Supreme Court held in a 5-4 ruling that the Second Amendment applies to state and local governments in addition to the federal government. To the extent that post-*Heller* courts have heard Second Amendment challenges to CCW laws, they have rejected those challenges. In any event, because strong CCW laws do not affect an individual's right to self-defense in the home—the core of the Second Amendment as interpreted in *Heller*—those laws should not conflict with the Second Amendment.

The gun lobby has succeeded in systematically weakening concealed carry laws across the country.

Common Sense Policies to Reduce the Risk of Carrying Concealed Weapons

In recent decades, the gun lobby has succeeded in systematically weakening concealed carry laws across the country: States that choose to permit the carrying of concealed weapons can reverse this trend by adopting the following common sense policies:

- A license or permit must be required in order for an individual to lawfully carry a concealed weapon.

- Law enforcement should have discretion to issue permits based upon a showing of a justifiable need. Persons convicted of a wide variety of weapons-related or violent misdemeanors should be prohibited from receiving CCW permits.

- In addition to background checks, applicants must be required to undergo safety training and to pass written and hands-on tests demonstrating knowledge of firearm laws and safety.

- Permits must be of limited duration (e.g., one or two years) and renewed only upon satisfaction of all application requirements, including a background check.

- Carrying concealed weapons should be permitted in only a limited number of public places. Carrying should be prohibited in at least the following locations: school property, establishments which serve liquor, places of worship, polling places, sports arenas, medical facilities, sites where gambling is permitted, public parks, and courthouses and other government buildings.

- A CCW permit holder should not be exempt from a background check when purchasing a firearm, despite a federal law that allows states to seek exemptions for qualifying permits.

LCAV is available to provide advice on legislation to implement any of these recommendations.

5

Concealed Weapons Protect Personal Freedoms

A.W.R. Hawkins

Dr. A.W.R. Hawkins is a columnist for Human Events, *a writer for Pajamas Media, and a Visiting Fellow at the Russell Kirk Center for Cultural Renewal.*

Following his 1994 gubernatorial victory in Texas, former president George W. Bush signed a "shall issue" concealed weapons bill into law allowing all applicants who met the requirements to obtain a concealed weapons permit. Critics of the law argued that incidents of violence would increase; however, proponents of the concealed weapons law insisted that crime rates would drop as they had in Florida, where crime rates fell forty percent after Florida legislators passed their own concealed weapons law in 1987. Laws permitting concealed weapons protect more than just the permit holder; concealed weapons protect the freedom of those around with the constant threat to criminals of a potentially armed citizen.

When I'm free, you're free. When we're free, they're free.

I live in the great state of Texas, the land of cowboys, guns, oil rigs, guns, pickup trucks, guns, recent U.S. Presidents, guns, the annual Houston Rodeo, guns, a [National Hockey League] franchise, a couple of [National Football League] franchises and, did I mention guns? Though gun ownership is a strong characteristic of American culture as a whole it is a predominant trait in Texas where it is rightly taken as a guarantee of freedom.

The would-be sexual predator must start guessing which female might have a .357 magnum in her purse . . . and which might not.

When President George W. Bush was running for governor of Texas in 1994, one of his campaign pledges was that if elected, he would pass the concealed carry law that then-governor Ann Richards refused to pass (and promised to veto). Bush won that election, and a law allowing Texas citizens to acquire a permit which would allow them to carry concealed handguns on their persons began its way through the state legislative chain. Subsequently, of course, every anti-gun activist within shouting distance of a telephone began calling media outlets and Texas politicians, predicting the "certain" bloodbath that would follow the implementation of the new ordinance. The truth, however, was another thing altogether.

Concealed Weapons Deter Criminals and Reduce Crime Rates

Amidst the frantic disinformation campaign by gun control proponents, the [National Rifle Association] and the Texas State Rifle Association asserted that concealed carry laws reduce crime and violence because they present would-be criminals with a serious problem: the problem of ascertaining who is and who is not armed. For example, once such a law is in place, the would-be sexual predator must start guessing which female might have a .357 magnum in her purse with which to defend her life and dignity, and which might not. The dilemma for such a thug is that if picks the wrong the woman, his life is over. That is quite a deterrent for anyone accustomed to breathing, eating, and sleeping, criminals included.

Bush, the NRA, the Texas State Rifle Association, and common sense had the facts on their side. Prior to Florida's passage of a similar concealed handgun law in 1987, the crime rate in the Sunshine State was a whopping 36% above the national average. I remember that time prior to 1987 vividly because my father, who used to take the family to Florida for vacation each year, decided to vacation elsewhere as a result of the literal onslaught of killings, burglaries, and other crimes being committed against tourists month after month in Florida's rest areas. But within four years of passing a concealed carry law, Floridians saw their crime rate plummet to 4% below the national average, according to David Kopel. Although my father never carried a gun in Florida, we began vacationing there again and benefited from the safety that resulted from other citizens carrying their concealed weapons.

When I carry a concealed handgun people around me ... are safer because of its deterring affect on the behavior of would-be criminals.

Concealed Weapons Protect the Public

This is a lesson that I have never forgotten: When I'm free, you're free. In other words, when I carry a concealed handgun, people around me who do not carry one, and who may not even know me, are safer because of its deterring affect on the behavior of would-be criminals.

This came to mind recently as I was watching a morning show on one of the Hispanic channels on television. Two women were hosting the show and providing a mixture of news and entertainment, an arrangement similar to Fox and Friends, Good Morning America, or any number of morning television shows in America. As I watched, my thoughts moved from noting how the Latino morning show imitated popular American culture to a similar, yet fuller realization: When we're free, they're free. The Latino hosts' laughter and frivolity, though taking place in a country less free than ours, takes place in country as free as it is because we are beside them, armed and ready; a quasi-permanent protective stance we took through the issuance of the Monroe Doctrine in the early 1800s [which prohibited European colonization in the Americas]. Their laughter was reminiscent of the laughter my parents and I shared on the Florida beaches, in a similar happy go-lucky existence that resulted from law-abiding citizens around us carrying guns they could to use to defend justice by stopping criminal aggression.

As this realization churned in my mind, I thought of other countries, the freedom of which is perhaps even more clearly tied to our freedom. Countries like Israel, Iraq, Taiwan, The Philippines, South Korea, Poland and other former Soviet satellites. When we're free, they're free.

Laws Opposing Concealed Weapons Cause a Rise in Crime

When opponents of concealed handgun laws protest because such laws will lead to bloodshed, rising crime rates, and increased "shoot outs" in the streets, they fail to take into the account the fact that the evidence is wholly and overwhelmingly against them. And most importantly, they fail to understand that whether they ever get a concealed gun permit or not, a gun concealed on my belt makes their children less likely to be targeted by criminals or pedophiles as they play with my children at the park. To put it another way, again: when I'm free, you're free.

When Leftists such as [businessman and political activist] George Soros or [President] Barack Hussein Obama decry our military might or seek to lessen if not destroy our status as the world's lone superpower, they do so at the very expense of those about whom they claim to be concerned. If we truly want children, families, and individuals the world over, but especially in the lands of our allies, to be safe and free, we must remember that when we're free, they're free.

Our status as sole possessors of certain weapons and armed forces in this world poses no threat to those who do not threaten us or our allies, and they allow our neighbors to the South to spend their weekday mornings laughing with Americanized television hosts instead of crawling into bomb shelters.

6

Concealed Weapons Infringe upon the Personal Freedoms of Others

Steve Chapman

Steve Chapman is a columnist and editorial writer for The Chicago Tribune.

In 2008, the Florida legislature passed a law allowing concealed weapons to be kept in permit holders' vehicles at their place of employment. Companies are forced to comply with this new legislation regardless of the remonstrations of business owners who, until this time, could decide whether to allow concealed weapons on their property. Business owners no longer have the right to ensure the safety and security of their property and employees, and those permit holders who do not drive to work are unfairly excluded from bringing their concealed weapons with them. Concealed weapons are not appropriate for every work environment, and business owners should have the right to decide whether they are comfortable with guns on their property.

Supporters of the right to keep and bear arms have long recognized the value of firearms for the defense of life, liberty, and property. But in Florida, a perverse conception of the 2nd Amendment has produced the opposite effect: The cause of gun rights is being used to attack property rights.

In 1987, Florida wisely affirmed personal freedom by letting law-abiding citizens get permits to carry concealed weapons. But this year [in 2008], the legislature decided it was not enough to let licensees pack in public places. They also should be allowed to take their guns into private venues—even if the property owner objects.

Bringing Guns into the Workplace

The "take your guns to work" law says anyone with a conceal-carry permit has a legal right to keep his gun locked in his car in the company parking lot. Until recently, companies had the authority to make the rules on their own premises. But when it comes to guns, that freedom is defunct.

A municipal government may not forbid guns to every-one on the territory under its control. But ... a private property owner certainly can.

The National Rifle Association [(NRA)] says any corporation that forbids firearms in its parking areas is violating the 2nd Amendment. That may sound like a promising argument, since the Supreme Court recently struck down a Washington, D.C., handgun ban as an infringement on the constitutional guarantee. It's not.

Robert Levy, the Cato Institute lawyer who participated in the successful challenge of the Washington ordinance, says the Florida law "has nothing to do with the 2nd Amendment." The Constitution, he notes, is a limit on government power, not a constraint on what private individuals or corporations may do.

Infringing on Property Rights

A municipal government may not forbid guns to everyone on the territory under its control. But, as far as the Constitution is concerned, a private property owner certainly can.

A federal court recently upheld the law, but not because of the Bill of Rights. It said that "the constitutional right to bear arms restricts the actions of only the federal or state governments or their subdivisions, not private actors," and noted that the NRA "has been unable to cite any authority for its position."

So the law doesn't uphold gun rights. What it does do is infringe on property rights. The Florida Chamber of Commerce makes the obvious argument that there is no right "to have a gun in your car on *someone else's property*" (my emphasis). But the law tells company owners they have no control over workers who insist on bringing deadly weapons onto their premises.

This is not a place where the government should substitute its judgment for that of the property owners.

Keeping Everyone Safe

Conceal-carry licensees complain that if they can't keep their guns in their cars, they will have no protection on their way to and from work. That's true. But what about employees who walk, bike, or take the bus? Since the law doesn't give them the right to take their guns into the workplace, they have to leave them at home. Should the state force companies to let workers carry pistols into the factory, office, or day-care center?

This is not a place where the government should substitute its judgment for that of the property owners. One lawyer told *The Bradenton Herald*, "I have clients that have to carry out terminations. Sometimes that termination is volatile. A lot of places have a policy where they walk the terminated employee to his car. What if you walk the guy to his car that has a gun? I wouldn't want to be that supervisor."

Given that crimes by permit holders are exceedingly rare, the employers who want to ban guns may be running from shadows. But decisions about their safety, and that of their customers and employees, should be theirs to make.

For some people, being temporarily deprived of a firearm creates great anxiety. But for those with a strong aversion to guns, working at a company that allows weapons in cars has the same effect. In a free society, both sets of employees can solve the problem with a simple expedient: exercising their liberty to find a company whose policies suit their preferences.

For the NRA to demand that guns be allowed in every company lot is just as oppressive as it would be for the Brady Center to Prevent Gun Violence to insist they be prohibited in every company lot. When gun-rights advocates oppose the use of government power to suppress firearms, they are advancing freedom. When they use government power to dictate to private companies, they are harming it.

7

National Standards for Concealed Weapons Are Necessary

Steve Henson

Steve Henson is the managing editor for the southern Colorado daily newspaper, The Pueblo Chieftain.

The process of obtaining a concealed license permit in Colorado involves a Colorado Bureau of Investigations background check, a thorough certified training class, and hands-on experience with properly handling concealed weapons which prepares the applicant for the responsibilities of carrying a concealed weapon; however, every state does not require such a rigorous process to obtain a permit. The creation of exacting national standards for concealed weapons would eliminate inconsistencies between states, ensure that proper certification was given to applicants, and prepare them for the charge of their concealed weapon.

The U.S. Senate last week [on July 21, 2009] rejected a proposal to allow anyone who has a state-issued concealed weapons permit to carry a hidden weapon in most other states. The arguments were fairly direct: One side contended that it would make interstate travel safer; the other argued that some states' permitting requirements are too lax, and as a result, there are too many people carrying hidden weapons who shouldn't be.

Obtaining a Concealed Weapons Permit

I found the story particularly interesting because I did something a few years ago that I previously never would have conceived of doing: I got a concealed weapons permit. Unlike most guys, I am not fascinated by guns. I wasn't raised around guns and the extent of my lifetime experience was firing a shotgun a couple of times as a teenager when I went pheasant hunting with one of my friends and his dad. Until a few years ago, I had never owned a gun. Never wanted to. They scared the hell out of me, and still do. But this is a crazy world we live in, and after a number of unrelated telephone calls from individuals upset with the newspaper for this or that, over a period of time, I convinced myself that it wouldn't hurt anything to get a permit and learn how to use a gun. Talk about clueless. Not knowing how to proceed, I asked some of my friends in law enforcement what to do. They wisely suggested that I apply for a permit because the process includes a significant training component. First, I was impressed by the application process. I applied with the Pueblo County Sheriff's Department, which required a Colorado Bureau of Investigations background check—it came back "ugly but not dangerous"—and a National Rifle Association [(NRA)]-certified training class. I wasn't crazy about that. I've often disagreed with what I believed to be extreme positions taken by the NRA. I learned, however, that, politics aside, the NRA does a very good job of training. I took a one-day, 13-hour, certified class from Puebloan Leonard Jimenez, and it was fantastic. He showed us how to handle and clean guns; we talked extensively about self-defense approaches; we heard from a police officer about how the law applies to self-defense and carrying concealed weapons; and finally, we actually took some guns to the shooting range in Pueblo West and fired them.

Standardize the Concealed Weapons Permit Process

I had to borrow one of his guns because I didn't own one at the time. Most of the people in the class were very experienced with guns and brought their own. But they were very patient and helpful with me, as was Jimenez, and at the end of the day, I had a pretty good start. I subsequently have been a member, off and on, of the Pueblo Municipal Shooters, and actually can hit a target fairly often. In reference to the law that was defeated, I would argue that I would feel a lot more comfortable driving from state to state with a gun in my car. I don't know about you, but I find lots of rest stops pretty unnerving. And if you drive enough, you'll have some strange experiences with other motorists. But I also see the point about registration and training. It would seem that a compromise would be fairly simple: Make the licensing federal and make it consistent. Eliminate the state-to-state inconsistencies. Don't allow fly-by-night outfits that offer a couple of hours of training then issue somebody a certificate. Make the training thorough. Do computerized background checks. When people reapply, make them demonstrate proficiency in handling a weapon and their understanding of their responsibilities. Raise the fees however high they need to be to pay for this bureaucracy. I'm not crazy about carrying a gun or knowing that other people are carrying them. I would prefer a country without guns. But I'd feel a lot safer knowing that a consistent and comprehensive permitting program were in place, rather than today's piecemeal approach that was illuminated in the recent Senate debate.

8

A Permit Should Not Be Necessary to Carry a Concealed Weapon

Clair Schwan

Clair Schwan is the founder of the website Libertarian-Logic.com, which explores the philosophies of libertarianism. He is an author and contributor for many websites that embrace a philosophy of self reliance, and he hosts Frugal-Living-Freedom.com, a website dedicated to helping others live a more self directed life, with an eye towards making the most out of hard earned money and living debt free. He was also a 2008 Libertarian Party Candidate to Wyoming's House of Representatives.

The federal and state governments use concealed weapons permits to control its citizens, though concealed weapons permits only serve to regulate those citizens who are law-abiding. Historically, gun control laws have been used to discriminate against former slaves and the non-wealthy. In many states, those who wish to obtain a concealed weapon permit must pay for the permit and receive a certificate of training. Individuals desiring a license are at the mercy of the state issuing the permit. The concealed weapons permit process does not deter criminals from obtaining guns or committing crimes; therefore, law-abiding citizens should not be required to apply for a concealed weapon permit. Unnecessary regulation of the right to carry a concealed weapon will lead to other rights being regulated and restricted.

W hat is a concealed weapons permit, what is it supposed to do, and is it really needed to help ensure our safety?

These are three good questions with really simple answers that I'll provide you with in this article.

Remember, you'll be getting answers from a Libertarian that believes in the natural right of self-defense, so be prepared for answers that resonate with freedom, rights and justice.

Let me answer these questions, and then offer discussion.

First, a permit to carry a concealed weapon is just another way your government attempts to control your behavior. It is a licensing of your right to bear arms, perhaps the only enumerated right that we openly license.

Second, the whole idea behind the concealed weapons permit process is to make certain that only the "good guys" are carrying concealed weapons among the general populace. It is designed to keep guns out of the hands of the "bad guys" and thereby prevent violent crime.

Third, the whole idea of a concealed weapons permit is absolutely unnecessary because the process only applies to the law abiding. As you'll probably come to agree, the law abiding are the ones who we shouldn't have concern about in the first place, so why try to regulate their actions?

In the following discussion, I'll use the terms concealed weapons permit, concealed carry permit and concealed firearms permit interchangeably. They are the same thing. The variation in terminology stems from how some law enforcement agencies in various states prefer to call their concealed weapons permit.

The History of Concealed Weapons Laws

Gun control has been with us for many generations. A concealed weapons permit is just another form of it. Let's look at three examples of gun control to see that regardless of the intentions, it really only punishes the innocent and law-abiding among us, and does nothing but benefit the criminally-minded.

Some of the early forms of gun control took the form of laws that forbade former slaves from owning firearms. This effectively disarmed a specific group of citizens so they would be defenseless in the face of racists and others that wanted to retain power and control over blacks.

In 1934, congress passed the National Firearms Act that required an application for a license and a tax of $200 to be paid before a citizen could own a machine gun. This was supposed to cut down on criminal use of machine guns, but as you can imagine, the $200 fee back in 1934 (when an apartment rented for $15 a month and cheese was 24 cents a pound) only deterred average citizens from owning a gun that could operate in a fully automatic mode.

The law abiding are penalized with fees and prohibitions while the criminals get all the weapons they care to pay for.

Some states prohibited ownership of machine guns, so even if you wanted to (legally) own one, you couldn't get a license if you were a resident of a state that prohibited them.

So, here we are 75 years later, and it isn't at all uncommon for criminals to have automatic weapons for their gang related enterprises (regardless of what state they live in.) So, history shows us once again that the law abiding are penalized with fees and prohibitions while the criminals get all the weapons they care to pay for.

Concealed Weapons Permits Vary by State

That brings us to the concealed weapons permit, something that nearly every state has in one form or another. Nearly 40 states have a "shall issue" law that requires no "need" be shown for a citizen to apply for the concealed carry permit.

A handful of states have concealed weapons permit programs based on a show of "need". Michigan used to be that way. You had to demonstrate that you carried cash as a part of your business, or were a woman alone at night as part of your employment requirements before you could get a local permit to carry a concealed firearm.

With the exception of Vermont, the law-abiding citizen must apply for permission to carry a weapon in self-defense.

States like Hawaii, California and New York have a concealed weapons permit process at either the state or local level based on "need", but they don't regularly issue permits. I understand that Hawaii hasn't issued a single permit.

Other states don't have a concealed weapons permit process because they don't allow concealed carry of deadly weapons. Wisconsin is such a state. This isn't a surprise when you consider that Wisconsin also has a law in place that says you can't discriminate against applicants for employment based on their arrest or conviction record.

I'm not liking the idea that a convicted bank robber, forger or counterfeiter has to be given equal consideration for a position in a bank right alongside of others who have no criminal record. But then, that's one of the reasons I don't live or work in Wisconsin.

Lastly, there's Vermont where they have no concealed weapons permit because there are no restrictions against concealed carry, unless you're doing it for unlawful purposes. Okay, so there is one state with a sane concealed carry law.

So, with the exception of Vermont, the law-abiding citizen must apply for permission to carry a weapon in self-defense. Usually this involves fees, training and issuance of an identification card. Oh, and I almost forgot to mention—it usually also requires that you wait until the state is ready to issue you the permit.

The Idea Behind the Concealed Weapons Permit Process

Okay, so the concealed carry process is a burden, an expense and an inconvenience. But it has an upside doesn't it? Well, supposedly, but I sure can't find it.

The law-abiding are faced with the restriction ... and the lawless are not.

The idea behind the permit process is to keep guns out of the wrong hands. Only those who "qualify" should have guns on the street, so why is it that criminals everywhere have guns if they so choose? The answer is simple, they pay for them on the black market.

I find it so ironic that the criminal underworld operates very much on the basis of free enterprise, whereas the free market economy operated in the light of day has many restrictions that cause it to be, well, not so very free after all.

In other words, the law-abiding are faced with the restrictions such as applications, training, fingerprinting and waiting for approval, and the lawless are not. This can hardly be the intention of such laws, but it's what we have in place.

So who is it that gets a concealed weapons permit?

Concealed Weapons Permits Only Regulate Law-Abiding Citizens

Simply put, the law-abiding are the ones who apply for a concealed weapons permit. This seems obvious to me, but then I'm familiar with the process. As a rule, criminals don't apply for the permit/license.

Even if criminals do apply, they won't be approved (if the process works correctly), so only the law-abiding will have a permit. Think about it. The law-abiding are the ones who we should not fear, and yet they are the ones who we are trying to regulate.

Criminals are indeed the ones we should fear, and yet they aren't regulated at all. At least, not until they commit a crime. Until that time, they would appear as any other law-abiding citizen on the street.

So, there you have it. We are imposing a regulatory burden on the law-abiding. This regulatory burden is indeed a penalty of sorts for being a law-abiding citizen.

The criminal has no such regulatory burden, unless they are apprehended during their involvement in a crime in which they are in possession of a concealed deadly weapon. Often-times, minor charges such as carrying a concealed deadly weapon are plea-bargained away in favor of prosecuting major offenses, or a criminal pleads guilty to the misdemeanor of concealed carry as a lesser offense in order to escape prosecution of the more serious crimes.

The Concealed Weapons Permit Process

I want to tell you about my experience with Wyoming's concealed carry process. I found it quite interesting. Wyoming law requires that you obtain training, submit fingerprints, and wait 60 days before being issued a concealed firearms permit (if you are indeed qualified under the program.)

I complied with all the requirements of the law, and then inquired as to the status of my permit after the 60 days had elapsed. I was told that I could not obtain the permit until my fingerprints had been returned from Washington.

I explained that the law required the state to issue me a concealed firearms permit at the end of 60 days, or write me a letter telling me why I didn't qualify. I was told that the state did not issue permits until the fingerprints came back from the FBI. I reminded the program clerk of the 60 day requirement, and she informed me that the state would not be "upstanding" if they issued permits before the fingerprint check had been completed.

Of course, the 60 day limitation is put in place because the delay in fingerprint processing could go on indefinitely. The state program clerk assured me "that has never happened." How reassuring, *indefinitely* has never happened.

So here we have a department within the Attorney General's office, the number one law enforcement officer in the State of Wyoming, and they are in direct violation of state law as a matter of course in program implementation. Moreover, their explanation for violating state law was that the Legislature had no idea how long it would take to get the fingerprint check completed.

(Oh, yes they did have an idea of the delays. That's why they placed a 60 day limit on issuing a concealed weapons permit.)

My overall impression was that the state felt somehow responsible for me and my actions, up to the point where they knew positively that it was okay to issue the permit. But, the state felt no obligation to protect me during the interim while they violated state law by not issuing my permit.

How odd, the state doesn't want to look bad by following the law, but had no problem with me being defenseless because of their decision to implement the program contrary to law.

Here we have a classic example of why laws should not be passed in the first place:

- they are misinterpreted

- they are deliberately misapplied

- they are enforced in imaginative and discretionary ways

- they only apply to the law-abiding

- we believe they will be followed by criminals

My solution to the problem with the Attorney General's office was rather simple. I informed the clerk that when I arrived back from my travels in another state, that I was going to open carry throughout the streets of Cheyenne and do all of my errands and business with a gun on my hip—including trips to the bank and the grocery store and strolling downtown.

I also informed her that if questioned by citizens, reporters or law enforcement, I would simply inform them that I have the gun in plain sight and within easy reach to be able to defend myself because the Attorney General's office has left me in a defenseless position, through their deliberate violation of state law when it comes to the concealed weapons permit process.

Some people think that having a permit to carry a gun is synonymous with having a license for murder, mayhem, and intimidation.

I was then informed by the state clerk (concerned mother figure that she is) that should I desire to carry a firearm openly, I should inform local law enforcement beforehand. Isn't that great? I have to inform law enforcement when I'm going to do something that is perfectly legal to do.

I suggested to her that perhaps I would inform local law enforcement each time I went out to do my laundry. Well, why not? Open carry in Wyoming is legal, and so is doing laundry.

All of this goes to show you that the law-abiding are burdened with the law, and the criminal is only burdened to the extent that they are caught in violation of the law.

Life with a Concealed Weapons Permit

My recommendations to you are very simple.

First, get a concealed weapons permit so you understand what it's like to have your rights licensed much like a privilege.

Get your training, have your fingerprints taken, pay the permit fees, and then wait for the license.

Next, conceal your weapon appropriately and go for a stroll down the street. Imagine that you're a criminal and not a law-abiding citizen. This will demonstrate to you know just how easy it is for an armed criminal to go about his or her day-to-day business among law-abiding citizens.

Keep track of your activities to see if you do the following:

- run around with your gun

- put your gun on the street

- draw your weapon in anger

- shoot at people over trivial matters

- injure or kill innocent children on a playground

- charge into a school on a shooting rampage

- commit other crimes such as armed robbery or kidnapping

It is amazing to me how some people think that having a permit to carry a gun is synonymous with having a license for murder, mayhem and intimidation.

I think you'll find that even after many years of carrying a concealed firearm, you rarely have the need to brandish the weapon, let alone use it. You'll also find that having the weapon in your possession in no way influences you to do things of a foolish or criminal nature.

As [American musician and gun rights proponent] Ted Nugent reminds us: "If guns cause crime, mine must be defective."

Also, remember to notify authorities of your changes of address, and periodically pay a fee to be reissued your permit to carry a concealed weapon.

Last but not least, be prepared to have other rights regulated, permitted, and otherwise turned into a privilege.

This Libertarian believes that there is only one sure way to stop this silly belief that we need a concealed weapons permit. That one sure way is simply to require training, licensing and permitting for:

- obtaining legal counsel

- going to church

- hanging out with your friends

- writing a letter to the newspaper

- lobbying your state or federal legislature

- having a trial by jury

I think that would finally ram home the point that many a Libertarian has been making for years: "What part of 'shall not be infringed' don't you understand?"

9

Permits Should Be Required for Concealed Weapons

Clayton E. Cramer

Clayton E. Cramer is a software designer and historian. His sixth book, Armed American: The Remarkable Story of How and Why Guns Became as American as Apple Pie, *was released in 2007.*

With the repeal of the law requiring concealed weapons permits for those over the age of 21, Arizona's new concealed weapons policies give cause for concern. Eliminating the need for concealed weapons permits may make it easier for those who are mentally unstable or irresponsible to carry concealed firearms, as lengthy applications, permit waiting periods, and permit training courses required by many states serve to potentially deter these applicants from obtaining a permit.

It has been another astonishing month for the right to carry. Arizona effectively "went Vermont." The state legislature repealed the requirement that those over 21 have a concealed weapon permit, with one apparent exception: you still need a permit to carry a concealed handgun into a place that serves alcohol. If the establishment has a prohibition of guns, you still can't enter while carrying. It appears that Arizona will continue to issue concealed carry permits, both for carrying in bars, and so that Arizonans can carry concealed in the more than 30 states that recognize Arizona permits.

Clayton E. Cramer, "Arizona Goes Vermont," *Shotgun News*, June 01, 2010. Reproduced by permission.

Concerns About Concealed Weapons Carriers

I've written before that I have some concerns about abolishing the requirement for a concealed carry permit. One of those concerns is political; opponents of shall-issue permit laws may use the passage of such laws in Alaska and Arizona as evidence of a deep dark conspiracy to repeal all gun laws. My flippant response is, "Only in states whose names start with A." The more thoughtful response is, "You mean slippery slopes really do exist? Not just in the direction of more restrictive gun control?" Since there are only a few states left that do not have shall-issue concealed weapon permit laws maybe I don't need to worry too much about this.

My other concern is that there are people for whom carrying a gun may not be wise. These are people who are not prohibited from owning a gun, but who are short-tempered, or who get drunk and stupid in public places, or are mentally unstable. They have not crossed the line into a prohibited category—and yet if we could find some way to discourage such a person from carrying a gun, it might be a good thing.

In the last 20 years, concealed weapon permits have gone from very difficult or impossible to get to pretty easy.

I think most of my readers know at least one person in this category: not quite irresponsible enough for the law to prohibit owning a gun, but someone who might benefit from a slight encouragement not to carry a gun.

Obviously, serious criminals are not going to let a permit requirement get in their way. Someone who intends murder, rape, or robbery, isn't going to let a concealed weapon permit stop him. But those are not the people that a concealed weapon permit law discourages from carrying a weapon. It's the guy who isn't a criminal—but who is not terribly responsible. If 20% of the population is in this category, and 10% of that 20% decides not to carry a concealed weapon without a permit, this could still be a net gain for civilized society.

Concealed Weapons Training

In the last 20 years, concealed weapon permits have gone from very difficult or impossible to get to pretty easy. The biggest obstacle in most of the U.S. now is the training requirement. While states that do not have those training requirements seem to do just fine, I confess that it does not bother me that someone has to sit in a classroom for a few hours and learn the legal requirements for use of deadly force. If this requirement, or having to fill out some paperwork and wait a few weeks for a background check is a big obstacle, perhaps this will cause some reflection about why you are carrying a gun.

All that said, this was the decision of the Arizona legislature to make. If they conclude, in a few years, that too many irresponsible persons are carrying concealed weapons to the detriment of public safety, I'm sure that they will change their law. I do find it interesting that Alaska made a similar decision to repeal its requirement for a permit several years ago, and has shown no signs of regret.

If the sheriff can provide specific examples of reasons to believe that this person is a danger to himself or others. . . the sheriff can still deny a permit.

Iowa's Shall-Carry Battle

As I write this column, Iowans are waiting to see it Gov. Chet Culver is going to sign SF 2379. Iowa for many years has had a discretionary concealed weapon permit law. Iowa sheriffs have largely unlimited discretion about issuance of concealed weapon permits—and predictably, some sheriffs have issued permits quite readily, while others have been quite restrictive.

SF 2379 takes away that discretion. It still allows a sheriff to deny a permit if "Probable cause exists to believe, based upon documented specific actions of the person, where at least one of the actions occurred within two years immediately preceding the date, of the permit application, that the person is likely to use a weapon unlawfully or in such other manner as would endanger the person's self or others."

A number of states have similar provisions. If the sheriff can provide specific examples of reasons to believe that this person is a danger to himself or others—say, because he spends a lot of time screaming at Martians—the sheriff can still deny a permit. But, "I don't think you need to carry a gun" isn't going to cut it.

The new law also defines what disqualifying actions prohibit receiving a permit, including any "serious or aggravated misdemeanor" as defined in existing Iowa law, and the usual prohibitions on gun ownership, such as felony convictions.

Permits are good for five years, and cost $50. A variety of classes meet the training requirement, including "any national rifle association handgun safety training course," an honorable or general discharge from the armed services, completion of basic training in the armed services, and a variety of security guard and law enforcement classes. The bill specifically prohibits sheriffs from requiring serial numbers or model numbers of weapons to be carried. In addition, the bill recognizes permits issued by other states for non-residents.

I suspect that by the time you read this column, Culver will either have signed or vetoed this bill. Since it passed both houses of the Iowa legislature with huge majorities (81-16 in the House, 38-4 in the State Senate), I expect that at some point, either this year or next, this is going to become law.

Twenty-five years ago, when I first became involved in the gun rights movement, I worried that we were engaged in a losing battle. No more!

UPDATE: As we went to press, Iowa Governor Culver announced that he would be signing the shall-issue concealed weapon permit law.

10

Weapons Laws Cause Police to Treat Permit Holders Like Criminals

Vin Suprynowicz

Vin Suprynowicz is the assistant editorial page editor of The Las Vegas Review-Journal.

Concealed weapons permit holders are treated like criminals simply for obeying the law. Unlike a criminal, who would not make law enforcement aware of a weapon that they are carrying, permit holders are required to inform law enforcement that they are in possession of a permit and weapon. Police officers put permit holders in unsafe situations by unnecessarily handcuffing them and stripping them of their legally permissible concealed carry weapon if they feel insecure or if they feel it is in the interest of their safety.

Charlie Mitchener is a 61-year-old general building contractor with an office near Patrick Lane and Fort Apache Road in Las Vegas. He holds permits allowing him to legally carry concealed weapons in Nevada, Florida and Utah.

Over the past three years [from 2007–2010], his office has been broken into five times. "Three of those occasions involved me interacting with Metro," he wrote to me recently. "Each of the occasions began the same: my introduction, my presentation of my Nevada drivers license and my concealed

Vin Suprynowicz, "Handcuffed, Disarmed for Obeying the Law," *Las Vegas Review-Journal*, January 10, 2010. Copyright © 2010 by Las Vegas Review Journal. Reproduced by permission.

firearms permit. Prior to today, each Metro officer simply replied thank you, proceeded with his work and then when complete there was a conversation about firearms."

Things were real different at 5:30 a.m, Jan. 3, however, when Mr. Mitchener called Metro to report the fifth break-in at his office.

"Vin, I hope I did not see the future this morning," Charlie e-mailed me. "Today was drastically different."

The responding officer was a lady cop, officer J. Rogers, badge number 13525.

Officers Put Concealed Weapons Permit Holders in Unsafe Situations

"Upon presentation of my (firearms permit), the officer asked if I had the weapon on me to which I replied yes. She then said to spread my legs and put my hands behind my back. I complied and she then handcuffed me. While doing so, she said that she wanted to make certain 'that we were all safe.'"

Officer Rogers stripped Mr. Mitchener of the Glock 19 he was carrying, took the weapon and locked it in her patrol car.

"Bear in mind that she had yet to clear my office (she was waiting for backup for clearing)," Charlie writes. "So, while remote, there was the possibility that the bad guys were still in my office and would come rushing out, finding me, to their delight, handcuffed. Apparently I was not included in her comment 'that we were all safe.' It is always nice when law-abiding citizens, particularly myself, are disposable.

"An hour or so later, when she had completed her paperwork, she came back in the office; I was in the rear and did not see her enter. She came to me and said that she had put my weapon in the second drawer on the left in the receptionist's desk.

"She then said that she could tell that I was upset with being handcuffed 'like a common criminal.' I explained that I was extremely upset and told her that it was out of respect to her that I provided my (firearms permit) and that the Second Amendment did have some meaning. She replied that the reason she did what she did was because she did not know if I was a bad guy or not. . . . I thought to myself, 'How absurd, I apply by the law to obtain permits, and yell it from the housetop that I have a permit and am carrying, just as I presume all bad guys do.'

"I asked if she was following procedure to handcuff me and remove my weapon to which she did not have a good answer, other than I was larger than her. . . . It certainly reminded me of the stories in New Orleans after [Hurricane] Katrina regarding confiscating weapons from the law-abiding citizens."

We should not be required to apply for any permit to carry a concealed weapon in the first place.

In the Name of Officer Safety

Another officer told Charlie that, based on J. Rogers' badge number, she had probably only been on her own for less than six months and was probably not secure in what she was doing. "It certainly makes me want to provide all the information the next time my office is broken into," he adds.

I talked to Charlie on Tuesday. He had called the concealed permit division that morning, and been referred to Internal Affairs, where he reports a detective told him, "It all depends on the officers, that if they think it's the safest thing to do they can do that. And he said it's best not to bring a weapon in this kind of situation."

Ah. So after going through all the rigmarole required to obtain a concealed weapons permit, it's best if a business owner who is the first to arrive at his office in the dawn hours to find it's been broken into *not* carry a weapon? Where the hell would the cops suggest would be a *better* circumstance into which to carry our legal self-defense weapon—a toddler's birthday party at Chuck E. Cheese?

I contacted Metro about this incident Tuesday. Late Friday, a spokesman confirmed Mr. Mitchener's account as "generally accurate," stating the officer "acted in a way that was in the interest of her safety."

Charlie Mitchener followed the law. He has trained at Front Site and with Tactical Response and continues to regularly visit the range. Yet, "In an instant, I am in handcuffs (at 61 years old, this was a first), and there were no bad guys in handcuffs with me, just the guy who thought he was doing things correctly," he writes.

We should not be required to apply for any "permit" to carry a concealed weapon in the first place. Despite this, Mr. Mitchener did everything required of him by law, ordinance and Metro instructions.

The Constitution does not say "the right to keep and bear arms shall not be infringed unless such infringement makes an officer of the government feel safer."

The officer handcuffed and disarmed him "so that everyone would be safe"? What a bunch of bull. If the burglar or burglars had emerged, they would have been confronted not by two armed law-abiding good guys, but instead by one small, frightened officer and a handcuffed and disarmed legal occupant. This rendered Mr. Mitchener "safer"?

Please note that if Mr. Mitchener had *not* followed law, ordinance, and Metro request, if he had carried a firearm in his waistband without ever seeking a permit or informing the officer he had it, the tiny officer would have had *no* probable cause to disarm him, and he would likely have remained armed throughout the entire encounter. Thus, he was punished, degraded, and treated like a common criminal *because and only because* he attempted to follow law, ordinance and Metro's legally dubious "instructions."

The cops don't get it. The Constitution does not say "the right to keep and bear arms shall not be infringed unless such infringement makes an officer of the government feel safer." The biggest reason the American populace are armed was never to fight off bears or wild Indians but to make agents of the government feel unsafe—really, really unsafe—should they try to take away our rights. That's why a citizen militia is "necessary to the security of a *free* state."

If these arrogant, uniformed employees of ours really want to treat us as the enemy, they may eventually get their wish, at which point they will discover they're vastly outnumbered— and "backup" is never quite close enough to solve the problem they've created for themselves.

America in 2025, gals: Keep at it, and it can be your own private Afghanistan.

11

Concealed Weapons Should Be Allowed on College Campuses

Theodore Day, Stan Liebowitz, and Craig Pirrong

Theodore Day is a professor of finance and Stan Liebowitz is the Ashbel Smith Professor of Economics, both at the University of Texas at Dallas. Craig Pirrong is a professor of finance at the University of Houston.

Mass public shootings almost exclusively occur in public places where concealed weapons are banned. Permitting concealed weapons on college campuses would reduce the incidence of violence, because concealed weapons permit holders could disarm or disable those who intend to do harm, and protect those that would otherwise become victims. Those who are licensed to carry concealed weapons commit less crime than the their fellow citizens, especially violent crime, assist in decreasing crime rates, and could potentially prevent mass shootings on campuses.

Mass public shootings are a horrific feature of modern life. Many of the bloodiest examples of this scourge have occurred on college campuses. As professors, we are particularly sensitive to this danger.

Despite this—no, because of this—we support [Texas legislation] that would permit the concealed carrying of firearms on college and university in the state by holders of concealed-handgun permits.

Any public policy involving matters of life and death should be decided only after weighing carefully the competing risks. Examining the relevant facts and data indicates that per-mitting Texas permit holders to carry weapons on college campuses would improve safety because:

- The best available empirical evidence shows that concealed-carry laws reduce the incidence of mass pub-lic shootings.

- Mass public shootings occur almost exclusively in places—like universities—where concealed carry is pro-scribed.

- There are numerous examples of firearms owners act-ing to disarm would-be mass murderers, thereby saving lives.

- Concealed-handgun-permit holders are overwhelmingly law-abiding individuals.

Gun-free zones are magnets for killers bent on maximiz-ing their body count.

Gun Bans Increase Instances of Multiple-Victim Crime

If gun bans truly reduced the risk of mass public shootings, then gun-free zones would be refuges from such havoc. Sadly, the exact opposite is true. All multiple-victim public shootings in the United States with more than three fatalities have oc-curred where concealed handguns are prohibited. Moreover, the worst primary and secondary school shootings have oc-curred in Europe, despite its draconian gun laws.

Furthermore, peer-reviewed research demonstrates that the passage of a concealed-carry law reduces incidents of mass public shootings. Tellingly, those episodes that have occurred in states allowing concealed carry overwhelmingly happened in places like schools and malls, where concealed carry was prohibited.

These facts should not be surprising. Gun-free zones are magnets for killers bent on maximizing their body count. They know that they face far less risk of quickly being stopped there. There are numerous cases in which private firearm owners have disarmed or disabled those attempting to murder indiscriminately in public places.

Texas permit holders commit misdemeanors and felonies at a rate of about one-seventh that of the rest of the population.

The Benefits of Concealed Weapons

In such circumstances, police officers and other "first responders" are anything but. The true first responders are often armed citizens who are in the line of fire. The possibility that a legally armed citizen could distract or disable an assailant could be the difference between life and death for potential victims.

Nor are the benefits of permitting concealed carry on campus limited to its effect on the likelihood of mass carnage. Numerous peer-reviewed academic studies document that concealed-carry laws reduce rates of violent crime. Therefore, extending the right to carry will also help reduce the rates of crimes against individuals that occur all too frequently in gun-free zones, such as college campuses.

On risks that concealed-carry licensees pose to their fellow citizens, the record is abundantly clear. Based on recent data, Texas permit holders commit misdemeanors and felonies at a rate of about one-seventh that of the rest of the population. For violent crimes, the rates are even lower.

Opponents of permitting concealed carry on campus raise concerns about guns in dormitories. These are misplaced. The bill would allow universities to prohibit weapon storage in dorms.

When concealed-carry laws were first proposed, opponents prophesied a plague of indiscriminate gunplay. It didn't happen. Similar apocalyptic fears are being raised now. The facts, though, demonstrate that concealed carry will reduce mass shootings.

As college professors, we want to reduce the odds of a Virginia Tech massacre happening on a Texas college campus. That's why we encourage the Texas Legislature to allow concealed carry on the state's college campuses.

12

Colleges Should Have the Authority to Ban Weapons from Campuses

Brian J. Siebel and Allen K. Rostron

Brian J. Siebel is a Senior Attorney of the Legal Action Project at the Brady Center to Prevent Gun Violence in Washington, D.C. Allen K. Rostron is an Associate Professor at the University of Missouri-Kansas City School of Law and a former Senior Staff Attorney at the Brady Center to Prevent Gun Violence.

Academic freedom can only be maintained if educational institutions are allowed to set their own policies concerning concealed weapons on college campuses. Introducing concealed weapons on campuses threatens academic freedom, creates an unsafe environment, and disrespects the property rights of the university. The majority of colleges and universities in the United States do not allow weapons on school grounds; however, in many areas of the country, legislation is being introduced that would take away an educational institution's right to ban weapons on campus.

"Academic freedom" is a vital, cherished concept in our Nation. It ensures that schools, teachers, and students can carry on all aspects of the educational process and pursuit of knowledge without undue interference.

Protecting free expression of teachers and students is the most obvious way in which academic freedom must be se-

Brian J. Siebel and Allen K. Rostron, "No Gun Left Behind," The Brady Center to Prevent Gun Violence, May 2007. Copyright © 2007 by The Brady Center to Prevent Gun Violence. Reproduced by permission.

cured. Teachers must be able to address even the most controversial subjects, in their research and writing endeavors as well as in the classroom, without fear that they will be punished for challenging conventional thought or espousing provocative ideas. Students must have the same ability to pursue knowledge without risk of being penalized or restrained by those who might disagree with the students' views. The Supreme Court of the United States has recognized that academic freedom has "long been viewed as a special concern of the First Amendment" and "is of transcendent value to all of us." It is thus an area in which government "should be extremely reticent to tread" and no "strait jacket[s]" should be imposed.

Schools should be given the authority and discretion to set policies that shape the academic environment in which teaching and learning will occur.

While free expression is tremendously important, academic freedom means more than simply letting teachers and students speak their minds. It also means respecting the need for academic institutions to be able to make independent decisions about the wide range of significant matters that surround the educational enterprise. Just as outsiders should not dictate what questions a teacher may ask or what answers a student may offer, schools should be given the authority and discretion to set policies that shape the academic environment in which teaching and learning will occur.

Academic Institutions Have the Legal Right to Control Policies on Their Campuses

The Supreme Court has recognized that academic freedom includes this institutional component, a right of universities to engage in "autonomous decisionmaking." Indeed, this "institutional right of self-governance in academic affairs" is the core principle endorsed in the Supreme Court's discussions of academic freedom.

Other courts have similarly recognized the importance of deferring to the decisionmaking and discretion of academic institutions. For example, when administrators at the University of Wisconsin suspended classes because of anti-war demonstrations in the early 1970s, courts recognized the importance of "[r]espect for the autonomy of educational institutions" and refused to overturn school officials' determinations about how best to ensure the safety of the academic community and to pursue the university's educational mission.

Academic freedom is not only a well-established legal principle, but also a strong cultural and professional norm in this country. The principal articulation of academic freedom principles, a statement issued by the American Association of University Professors in 1940, has been endorsed by hundreds of scholarly groups and every major higher education organization in the Nation. Recent decades have seen a movement toward consistently greater legislative recognition of and respect for the importance of autonomy for educational institutions.

This principle of institutional autonomy has even been enshrined in the constitutions of many states. For example:

- Alabama's Constitution provides that the state's university shall be under the management and control of its board of trustees.

- California's Constitution gives the Regents of the University of California "full powers of organization and government, subject only to such legislative control as may be necessary" to insure financial security and compliance with the terms of endowments and competitive bidding procedures.

- Florida's Constitution provides that the statewide board of governors shall operate, regulate, control, and be fully responsible for the management of the whole university system, subject to the legislature's powers to appropriate for the expenditure of funds.

- Georgia's Constitution states that the government, control, and management of the state's university system and all institutions within it shall be vested in the system's board of regents.

- Idaho's Constitution assigns the responsibility for general supervision of the university to the school's regents.

- Michigan's Constitution gives each board of regents the power of general supervision over the institution.

- Mississippi's Constitution assigns responsibility for the management and control of the state's institutions of higher learning to a board of trustees.

- Missouri's Constitution provides that government of the state university system shall be vested in the board of curators.

- Nevada's Constitution declares that the state's university shall be controlled by a board of regents.

- North Dakota's Constitution gives the state's board of higher education full authority over the state's educational institutions, including power to delegate to its employees the details of administration of the institutions.

- Oklahoma's Constitution vests the government of the state's university in a board of regents.

In one instance, a court has ruled that a state legislature deprived its universities of discretion to establish their own policies with respect to firearms. In that case, the court found that the Utah legislature had specifically opted to override the University of Utah's autonomy and its rule prohibiting its students, faculty, and staff from possessing firearms on campus. The court went out of its way, however, to emphasize that Utah provided an abnormally low measure of autonomy to its universities, compared to other states. Unlike other state constitutions, such as those mentioned above, Utah's Constitution assigns responsibility for "general control and supervision of the higher education systems" to the state legislature rather than to a governing body such as a board of regents or trustees. The Utah court also emphasized that it was not deciding whether the Utah legislature's action violated Federal constitutional guarantees, and that its decision should not be taken as suggesting that the state legislature made a wise decision in disregarding traditional principles of autonomy for educational institutions.

Firearm policies raise very significant and special issues for schools, as they have the unique mission of imparting learning and advancing knowledge.

Academic freedom thus remains a significant American value, reflected in law, tradition, and contemporary practice throughout the Nation. Institutional autonomy, including authority to make significant policy decisions, lies at the heart of academic freedom.

Guns Threaten Academic Freedom

A school's autonomy and independent decisionmaking authority should include the right to set policies concerning the presence of guns on campus. Possession of firearms at a school is a significant safety issue, as well as an important factor in the educational atmosphere created in an academic environment, over which a school should have control.

Firearms policies raise very significant and special issues for schools, as they have the unique mission of imparting learning and advancing knowledge. Each school strives to create a secure and constructive environment in which its educational mission can best be accomplished. As Justice Felix Frankfurter explained, "[i]t is the business of a university to

provide that atmosphere which is most conducive to specula-
tion, experiment and creation."

That objective brings with it a responsibility to regulate
the behavior of students, faculty, staff, and visitors in ways
that not only promote safety, but also promote the achieve-
ment of educational goals. The Supreme Court's Chief Justice
Earl Warren correctly observed that "[s]cholarship cannot
flourish in an atmosphere of suspicion and distrust." Likewise,
while sitting on the U.S. Court of Appeals for the Eighth Cir-
cuit before joining the Supreme Court, Harry Blackmun recognized that college regulations of students' conduct are "part
of the educational process itself" and that a school should
have "latitude and discretion in its formulation of rules and
regulations and of general standards of conduct."

A school could reasonably conclude that fostering the appropriate atmosphere for education would not be served by
allowing students to carry guns to class or permitting professors to arm themselves for faculty meetings. A school's decision should be respected to the extent that it determines, in
the exercise of its discretion, that it should restrict or prohibit
possession of guns at school.

Forcing Guns onto Campuses Violates Property Rights

Denying a private school the ability to make its own decisions
about firearms would be particularly inappropriate because it
would infringe on the school's authority as property owner.
The right to own and control one's own property is virtually a
sacred aspect of American law and culture. From the time
when America obtained its independence, private property
rights have been treated as a fundamental aspect of freedom.
For example, Arthur Lee, a member of the Continental Congress, proclaimed that "[t]he right of property is the guardian
of every other right." Likewise, as they headed into battle,
George Washington reminded his troops that they were fight-

ing to determine "whether they are to have any property they can call their own." Alexis de Tocqueville observed that "[i]n no other country in the world, is the love of property keener or more alert than in the United States, and nowhere else does the majority display less inclination toward doctrines which in any way threaten the way property is owned."

The Bill of Rights provided protection to property rights through the Fifth Amendment, which guaranteed that people would not be deprived of their property rights without due process of law and that just compensation would be paid for any government taking of private property for public use. Consistent with that, the Supreme Court has recognized that "government can scarcely be deemed to be free, where the rights of property are left solely dependent upon the will of a legislative body, without any restraint. The fundamental maxims of a free government seem to require, that the rights of personal liberty and private property should be held sacred."

No reasonable school administrator or campus security officer would want students or faculty to be armed.

Defying this fundamental tradition of respect for property rights . . . the gun lobby recently has been pushing for passage of "forced-entry laws" that would force property owners to permit possession of guns on their property. The American Bar Association, among others, has condemned the gun lobby's campaign and forced-entry laws as an improper infringement of traditional property rights of employers and other private property owners. "Forced entry laws deprive employer businesses and other property owners of their fundamental right to exclude individuals who possess firearms from their property," the ABA report found, and "such laws place substantial burdens on employer businesses by subjecting them to the risks associated with firearms in their workplaces without due process."

The gun lobby's campaign to push guns into schools and campuses also raises property rights concerns. Unlike businesses, which control property as private enterprises, most educational institutions in this country are public entities under some level of state control. However, private schools are in the same position as other businesses to set firearms policy on their property. Should the gun lobby seek to push laws like Utah's across that threshold, it will be invading the centuries-old tradition of respect for private property.

A climate of learning and free discussion and debate is not fostered when some of the people in classrooms have guns.

Tight Regulation of Firearms on Campuses Is Necessary

The smart choice by educational institutions—and one apparently made by nearly all schools and colleges—is a policy that bans or tightly controls firearms. It is the only policy that gives control to those responsible for the safety of students, faculty, staff, and visitors.

No reasonable school administrator or campus security officer would want students or faculty to be armed. Education professionals understand the risks on college campuses—alcohol and drugs, suicide and mental health issues, gun theft risks, and accidental shootings—that would be exacerbated if guns were introduced. They also understand why it is not a good idea to arm teachers. Moreover, they understand that a climate of learning and free discussion and debate is not fostered when some of the people in classrooms have guns. These are just some of the reasons why the University of Utah, for example, took its case all the way to the Utah Supreme Court and filed a separate Federal lawsuit to defend its no-guns policy.

It is only the people *not* responsible for school safety or guarding academic freedom that favor turning schools into armed camps. The Utah legislature has no responsibility for the safety of anyone that attends or visits school campuses. Slavish obedience to the wishes of the gun lobby appear to drive that legislature's choices, not student, or even public, safety.

Educational and law enforcement professionals agree that a policy tightly restricting or banning firearms on campus should be an essential part of every school security plan.

- The International Association of Chiefs of Police recommends suspending or expelling students that possess firearms on school property or at school events.

- The National Education Association recommends a clear and strictly enforced code that guns are not tolerated on school grounds. "A 'Zero Tolerance' policy is acceptable in these cases."

- The American Council on Education and several other higher educational institutions have written: "A university's decision to prohibit firearms on campus creates a secure, educational environment that ensures that the university's mission, the educational process and the quality of higher education can thrive—for the benefit of the entire academic community and the public good."

With a policy that tightly controls guns or bans them altogether, colleges and schools can ensure that the only people carrying guns are their security guards and the police. This is the way it has likely always been, and schools are safer because of it. For maximum safety and security, this is the way it should always be.

Protecting the Rights of Educational Institutions

Now is the time to take action to protect the rights of educational institutions to keep guns off campus. Unfortunately, those legal rights are now under attack by the gun lobby. The gun lobby is not known for issuing idle threats, and it has certainly made clear that it intends to push hard for arming students and teachers. Indeed, barely a week after the massacre at Virginia Tech, there is already a bill introduced in South Carolina that would permit anyone with a [carrying a concealed weapon, or] CCW license to carry a concealed weapon "on the premises or property owned, operated, or controlled by a public school, elementary school, secondary school, college, university, technical college, or other post-secondary institution." The bill would repeal existing South Carolina law that expressly prohibits CCW licensees from carrying guns into schools.

However, if educational institutions and communities band together in opposition to these laws, they can likely be stopped. Faced with the gun lobby's threat to pass legislation prohibiting employers from barring guns on company property, the business community has organized strong opposition in nearly every state where legislation has been proposed. The result has been a series of resounding defeats for the gun lobby. There is no reason that all of the people and institutions that run or support schools should not be similarly successful.

Institutions that educate and protect our children should not have their legal rights trampled by organizations promoting an extremist agenda. We need to make society safer by reducing easy access to guns by criminals, and mentally ill, unstable, or suicidal people, not make our schools more dangerous by making guns more accessible in colleges and schools.

13

Concealed Weapons Should Be Permitted in National Parks

David Kopel

David Kopel is the Research Director for the Independence Institute in Golden, Colorado, and an Adjunct Professor of Advanced Constitutional Law at Denver University's Sturm College of Law. Kopel is an Associate Policy Analyst for the Cato Institute, a Contributing Editor for Liberty *and* Gun Week *magazines, and the author of several books concerning gun rights and the constitution, including his latest book in December 2009,* Aiming for Liberty: The Past, Present, and Future of Freedom and Self-Defense.

Many Americans oppose new legislation allowing concealed weapons in national parks, and some opponents have stated that they will no longer visit national parks as a result of the law. Clinically speaking, a person who began to avoid or cease performing a regularly enjoyed activity, such as visiting national parks because of a hatred or fear of a specific object, in this case guns, has a phobia. This specific phobia, hoplophobia, would also cause one to avoid all places where guns are allowed. Since the majority of states in the U.S. allow concealed weapons, it is difficult to avoid areas where concealed weapons are legal when travelling within in the United States. Forty out of fifty states trust their residents to carry concealed weapons; allowing concealed weapons in national parks is a natural extension of this same trust and will not threaten the safety of other park patrons.

David Kopel, "Guns in Parks: The Hoplophobes' Travel Guide to the United States," *The New Ledger,* May 29, 2009. Copyright © 2009 by The New Ledger Publishing Company. Reproduced by permission.

Last week [On May 22, 2009], President [Barack] Obama signed a bill which, besides changing credit card laws, says that in National Parks and National Wildlife Refuges, the laws about gun carrying will be the same as in the host state. So in Colorado, for example, you will be allowed to carry a concealed handgun in Rocky Mountain National Park, if you have a state-issued concealed carry permit. In Vermont's Marsh-Billings-Rockefeller National Historical Park, you can carry at will, since no permit is required for carry in the rest of Vermont. In New Jersey' Gateway National Recreation Area, you will need a permit, and since almost no-one in New Jersey except retired police is ever granted a permit, almost no-one will be able to carry there.

The law goes into effect nine months hence, as do the changes in credit card laws.

Even the strongest scholarly advocates of gun control acknowledge that there are about a hundred thousand defensive gun uses annually.

Arguments Against Guns in National Parks

I was one of seven authors whom the *New York Times* invited to contribute a short essay on the new law, for the *Times*' online opinion feature, Room for Debate. All seven essays, from diverse pro/con viewpoints, were pretty good, I thought. The comments from readers, however, were voluminous but often very weak. Many of them consisted of left-over talking points from the gun control debate circa 1971, with assertions that no serious scholar of the gun issue believes. For example, many commenters claimed that it is impossible to use a gun in self-defense, because the attacker (whether a human or an animal) will have the element of surprise, that ordinary people are not competent to use guns for protection, and so on. Yet even the strongest scholarly advocates of gun control acknowledge that there are about a hundred thousand defensive gun uses annually, according to the National Crime Victimization Survey, which is conducted by the Census Bureau and the United State Department of Justice. (Other scholars argue for higher figures, but the key point is that no informed scholar claims that successful defensive use is rare or non-existent.)

Surprisingly, some of the commenters showed signs of mental illness. One commenter wrote that if he saw someone in a National Park with a gun, he would report the person for making criminal threats. ("Well, watch out, gunnut gunwack gunsels. If I see your gun while I am visiting the parks, I will file a complaint accusing you of threatening me.")

Now perhaps that commenter himself is just an ordinary criminal, and for many years has been breaking the law by making false accusations against innocent people. On the other hand, the commenter might not have been intending to make a knowingly false report, but instead to have been accurately predicted what he, with complete sincerity, would do. A person's belief, without a sufficient basis, that other people are committing crimes against him, is a symptom of Paranoid Personality Disorder.

An Irrational Fear of Guns in Parks

The more common form of apparent mental illness among some commenters was Hoplophobia, which is described in the book *Contemporary Diagnosis and Management of Anxiety Disorders*. A word of explanation: having a strong dislike or hatred of something is not, in itself, an indication of mental illness. For example, a person hates frogs, considers them disgusting, tries to avoid looking at frogs or touching them, and writes letters to the editor urging that all frogs be exterminated. This is not per se a sign of mental illness. Poor judgment, perhaps, but not a mental disorder.

So the vast majority of people who hate frogs, snakes, spiders, dogs, cats, guns, animals, George Bush, or anything else are *not* mentally ill.

Something becomes a specific Phobia, clinically speaking, when it significantly interferes with ordinary life activities. For example, "I turned down a job offer as a ticket-taker at the Natural History Museum, because I am afraid if I might see a child carrying a plush frog toy that was purchased in the museum gift shop." Or, "I refuse to visit my son who is a chef in a French restaurant, because I know that he has handled frog legs, and I terrified that he might shake my hand."

The new federal law simply means that the rule inside federal parks will be the same as in the host state.

Among the *New York Times* commenters, there were plenty of gun haters, the large majority of whom exhibited no sign of mental illness. Yet several of them wrote that they often visit national parks, enjoyed the visits, but now, because of the new federal law, they would not set foot in a National Park.

Now, as my *Times* essay had explained, and other commenters had reiterated, the new federal law simply means that the rule inside federal parks will be the same as in the host state. So the odds of running into a person legally carrying a firearm at, say, the Johnstown Flood National Memorial in Pennsylvania would be pretty close to the odds running into a legally armed person while walking down the streets of Johnstown, Pennsylvania.

In other words, someone who avoids National Parks because of the new law is saying that he is afraid of being in [a] place where most of the adult population has the legal right to carry a firearm, after licensing, a background check, and safety training. Meaning, of course, 40 of our 50 states.

Having so much hatred, or fear, of guns that you can't handle the ordinary, daily conditions of 4/5 of the American states would imply a rather significant interference with ordinary activities. That is, a phobia. The specific name for this phobia is "Hoplophobia." Although Hoplophobia would be a good name for fear of hopping animals such as frogs and kangaroos, the word's root is "hoplon"—from an ancient Greek shield that could be used offensively or defensively.

Hoplophobia

A caveat on the diagnosis: The American Psychiatric Association's *Diagnostic and Statistical Manual of Mental Disorders* includes, as part or the diagnosis for a phobia, that "The person recognizes that the fear is excessive or unreasonable. Note: In children, this feature may be absent." That condition is not met by the *New York Times* commenters, who appear to see themselves as eminently reasonable, and to consider anyone who would carry a firearm for protection as self-evidently crazy and dangerous. I don't think that the diagnosis of a phobia should require insight on the part of the phobic. If a person won't go to public places because he is afraid of balloons, then he would have a phobia, even if he considered himself eminently rational, and could recite statistics about all the people who have been seriously injured by balloons. (As was one of my relatives, when a Mylar balloon in a department store popped, and left her blind in one eye.)

Generally speaking, a mentally ill person has a better chance of being cured if he wants to be cured, and so the first step towards mental health is recognizing that one is mentally ill. So in the interest of perhaps encouraging some Hoplophobes to admit that they have a problem, here is a travel guide to the United States, based on the presumption that a person refuses to go any place where most adults can lawfully carry firearms for protection.

Places with Concealed Carry Laws Are Hard to Avoid

For convenience's sake, let's presume that the victim of Hoplophobia lives in Manhattan. Of course most people in Manhattan, including most Manhattanites who hate guns, are not Hoplophobes. But the island is a place to which Hoplophobes often migrate, perhaps as a form of self-treatment, trying to place themselves in a place where their phobia is less likely be triggered.

So starting in Manhattan, you can enjoy the entire Empire State, a large and interesting place. If you feel a desire to leave New York, be extremely careful about heading east. Going into Connecticut will immediately put you in a place where the government routinely issues carry permits to law-abiding, trained adults. In other words, Connecticut is just as danger-ous as a National Park.

Vermont is even worse, with no permits even required for carrying concealed handguns. And everyone knows how dan-gerous Vermont is. New Hampshire and Maine are similar to Connecticut, and must be avoided.

Massachusetts is safe, as long as you cross directly into the state, without going through Connecticut. Rhode Island is good too, providing that you approach it via Massachusetts, or take a ferry from eastern Long Island. A trip through Con-necticut would obviously be too risky.

New Jersey is the Hoplophobe's Garden State. Its licensing practices are much more severe than New York City's. In New Jersey, not even diamond merchants or celebrities can get carry permits.

From New Jersey, you must go south to Delaware. Do not even think of crossing into Pennsylvania. It is a Shall Issue state for carry licenses, similar to Maine or New Hampshire.

Maryland is also safe, and from there you can go to the District of Columbia, whose very strict gun laws have made it notoriously safe.

If you want to fly to D.C., take a plane to the Baltimore airport, and then rent a car or take a bus. Do not fly to either of the D.C. airports. They are both located in Virginia, and the danger that you could be shot by a gun-crazy Virginian while traveling through Virginia into D.C. is nearly as high as the odds that you will get shot by a gun nut while in a National Park. Stay away from Arlington National Cemetery; it is in Virginia, and the people buried there were gun users.

Needless to say, the entire Southeast is off limits. So is almost everything from Pennsylvania west. It is OK to fly to Illinois, and enjoy that state, since it does not even have procedures for issuing carry permits. The South Side of Chicago is an especially safe place to go, thanks to the handgun ban in the city.

Like Illinois, Wisconsin has no provision for handgun carry licenses, and so was safe until 2005, when the state Supreme Court ruled that people had a constitutional right to keep and carry guns in their place of business. After that, you could still go to Wisconsin, as long as you never entered a place of business. But now, the state Attorney General has advised that people have a right to open carry without a permit, and thus the Badger State is far too dangerous to contemplate a visit.

So is all the rest of the Midwest. So are all the Rocky Mountain states. So is the entire Southwest.

The Pacific Coast is mixed. Washington and Oregon are Shall Issue states. Alaska allows carry without a permit, and besides that, the mere thought of [former governor] Sarah Palin can trigger anxiety attacks in Hoplophobes.

California is safe, except for some of the rural counties, where sheriffs issue permits to law-abiding citizens. Permits are close to non-existent in Los Angeles, making South Central L.A. an especially safe area for the Hoplophobe.

Permits are also hard to get in Hawaii. So you can visit Haleakala National Park without worrying that someone on the trail up the volcano may have a gun.

In addition, New York's airports are gateways to the world, and you can travel to many global locations which are even stricter than New York City in their restrictions on gun ownership. You may find Cuba, Darfur, and North Korea to be especially pleasant places.

14

Concealed Weapons Should Not Be Allowed in National Parks

Todd Wilkinson

Todd Wilkinson has been an environmental journalist for twenty-five years and has been a contributor to many national magazines and newspapers. He is author of the critically-acclaimed book, Science Under Siege: The Politicians' War on Nature and Truth, *and he is the Editor-in-Chief of* Wildlife Art Journal.

Concerns are rising from park officials and various environmental groups about legislation that allows those with concealed weapons permits to carry their weapons into national parks. Legislation permitting firearms in national parks is polarizing and attempts to paint its opponents as being totally opposed to guns. Allowing concealed weapons in national parks will increase the potential for violent offenses such as poaching as well as create an environment that discourages those who are uncomfortable with their presence.

Always, the first question responsible legislators should ask when writing a law is this: What significant problem is being solved by putting another code on the books?

This is the nut of a conundrum now before the U.S. National Park Service as it prepares to deal with a new gun law buried as a rider (amendment) in a hastily-passed credit card reform bill on Capitol Hill.

It caught many by surprise. Public Law 111-24 will allow tourists, beginning in 2010 if not sooner, to openly tote the legal gun of their choice through national parks such as Yellowstone, Grand Teton and other bustling crown jewel preserves.

Rangers are deeply concerned about how the potential, expanded presence of firearms in crowded parks will affect human behavior.

In contrast to how the legislation was originally proposed, it is not a provision that only empowers licensed individuals with concealed weapons permits.

In some states, it allows any citizen, of legal age, to holster a loaded sidearm or walk with a rifle or shotgun slung over their backs through campgrounds, along hiking trails and while standing off roadways at popular scenic overlooks.

Tourists will even be able to use their riflescopes, while still on the barrel, as optical devices for viewing wildlife. As one seasoned professional with a state game agency told me: "It really opens up some mind-bending dilemmas, doesn't it?"

Rising Concerns

Park officials nationwide say they are committed to enforcing all laws handed down by Congress and the president.

But privately, rangers are deeply concerned about how the potential, expanded presence of firearms in crowded parks will affect human behavior in places where guns, for the most part, have not existed before, and where public and wildlife safety have not heretofore been problems in need of fixing.

Environmental groups such as the National Parks Conservation Association, the Natural Resources Defense Council, and the Greater Yellowstone Coalition have all warned of dire consequences. They are not anti-gun; they just believe the tradition of not having armed national park tourists, which has worked well for nearly a century, should be upheld.

Polarizing Legislation

Although the law was packaged in the flowery rhetoric of "expanding liberty" and protecting Second Amendment rights when first drafted during the Bush [George W.] Administration, it is, when one looks deeper, little more than a calculated wedge issue that only inflames our fear of each other.

I have never, after hiking thousands of miles and visiting dozens of national parks, ever felt the need to carry a loaded firearm inside one.

Authored by U.S. Sen. Tom Coburn (R-Oklahoma) and endorsed by the National Rifle Association [(NRA)] it is a thinly veiled attempt to create a false "pro-gun versus anti-gun" litmus test aimed at further polarizing the country.

I too own guns, and support and defend the right to bear arms that is a boilerplate component of the U.S. Constitution. I even firmly agree with the NRA on certain issues. But I have never, after hiking thousands of miles and visiting dozens of national parks, ever felt the need to carry a loaded firearm inside one.

Proponents say it will "protect Americans against violent crime", the kind that exists in urban parks and remote preserves along the U.S. border with Mexico. That may be.

But tell us, Senator Coburn, how many homicides, drug killings, and acts of gang violence have occurred in Yellowstone and Grand Teton in the last decade?

Name one.

Increasing the Likelihood of Violence

Fact: Nearly all of the violent offenses ever involving people and guns in these parks were carried out by poachers killing animals and not as acts of self-defense. One wonders: Has Coburn not been to Yellowstone?

Another thing he won't find in the Yellowstone and Grand Teton statistics are deaths or serious injuries caused by accidental gun discharges during the busy summer months. This law will actually increase the likelihood of that happening.

One can also imagine these scenarios: A family approaches a bison. A lone bull, say 40 yards away, raises his head and apart from roiling of tail, shows no indication of an imminent charge.

Is papa with a gun cleared of wrongdoing when he tells investigating rangers he shot and killed the bison because he was afraid the animal was about to trample a family member?

Or what about the autumn chaos that ensues when tourists and photographers swarm around bugling elk? In recent years, a few bulls have charged people who got too close. Will it now be acceptable to provoke an animal and then gun it down?

Or picture rangers pulling up alongside suspicious looking individuals standing near a steamy elk or bison or wolf carcass, fitting the profile of poachers, only to claim their lives were endangered?

Guns Will Discourage Visitors

Even more importantly, how will the presence of guns compromise the welcoming ambiance that three million visitors seek during their visits to Yellowstone and Grand Teton?

How will parents feel about paranoid individuals sitting around adjacent campfires with guns, leaning them up against their RVs or bringing weapons with them to outdoor ranger interpretive programs?

Apparently, handguns, rifles and shotguns will not be allowed in visitor centers, but there is a question about whether the prohibition applies to park hotels and restaurants where alcohol is served.

Public Law 111-24 does not enhance public appreciation for the Second Amendment; it is a liability to it.

If, and when it results in just one headline grabbing human tragedy or leads to an increase in wildlife poaching, will politicians who voted for it hold themselves accountable?

Organizations to Contact

The editors have compiled the following list of organizations concerned with the issues debated in this book. The descriptions are derived from materials provided by the organizations. All have publications or information available for interested readers. The list was compiled on the date of publication of the present volume; the information provided here may change. Readers need to remember that many organizations take several weeks or longer to respond to inquiries.

Arming Women Against Rape & Endangerment (AWARE)
We Are AWARE, Bedford, MA   01730-0242
phone: (781) 893-0500
e-mail: info@aware.org
website: www.aware.org

Founded in 1990, Arming Women Against Rape & Endangerment is an organization which promotes the education of personal safety and self-defense and provides training, information, and support to individuals, primarily women, on how to protect oneself if faced with a violent situation. AWARE is a non-profit organization whose mission is to prevent violence through education and training, and works with law enforcement, social workers, and various other groups to provide support for those in need. AWARE's website provides information for enrolling in their many gun safety and self-defense courses, crime statistics, articles and techniques for self protection, and offers advice and referrals for those in need of legal or personal assistance.

Citizens Committee for the Right to Keep and Bear Arms (CCRKBA)
Liberty Park, Bellevue, WA   98005
phone: (425) 454-4911
website: http://ccrkba.org

As an independent organization since 1971, The Citizens Committee for the Right to Keep and Bear Arms believes that the second amendment of the United States Constitution guarantees all citizens the right to keep and bear arms. CCRKBA believes that gun-control measures such as registration contribute to an increase in crime, confiscation of private citizens' weapons, and a loss of individual freedoms. Resources on CCRKBA's website include extensive coverage of gun rights issues and laws, congressional contact information, and recommended publications for further exploration of firearm rights.

Coalition for Peace Action (CFPA)
40 Witherspoon Street, Princeton, NJ 08542
phone: (609) 924-5022
e-mail: cfpa@peacecoalition.org
website: www.peacecoalition.org

The Coalition for Peace Action is a grassroots organization dedicated to the global abolition of nuclear weapons, the establishment of a peace economy, and a halt to domestic and international weapons trafficking. The CFPA has both a Political Action Committee that organizes lobbying and demonstrations, and the Peace Action Educational Fund that organizes peace conferences, concerts, and training in non-violent conflict resolution. News, CFPA events and campaigns, and information about CFPA's history and accomplishments can be found on their website.

Coalition to Stop Gun Violence (CSGV)
1424 L Street NW, Suite 2-1, Washington, DC 20005
phone: (202) 408-0061
website: csgv@csgv.org

Based in Washington, DC, the Coalition to Stop Gun Violence is a coalition of 48 national organizations who seek to end gun violence in the United States through research, strategic engagement, and effective policy advocacy. CSGV articles, research findings, and campaign information, as well as, press releases, gun control blogs, and congressional contact information are available on CSGV's website.

Gun Owners of America (GOA)

8001 Forbes Pl. Suite 102, Springfield, VA   22151
phone: (703) 321-8585
website: http://gunowners.org

Founded in 1975 by Senator H.L. Richardson, Gun Owners of America is a non-profit lobbying organization that promotes and defends the gun rights of private citizens under the Second Amendment of the United States Constitution. GOA's attorneys have provided legal counsel in gun rights related cases across the country. On their website, GOA provides extensive coverage of congressional debate, legislation, and voting records, ratings of congressional members, press releases, op-eds, bookstore, and video library, as well as many other resourses.

Jews for the Preservation of Firearms Ownership (JPFO)

P.O. Box 270143, Hartford, WI   53027
phone: (262) 673-9745 • fax: (262) 673-9746
e-mail: jpfo@jpfo.org
website: www.jpfo.org

Since 1990, Jews for the Preservation of Firearms Ownership has provided articles, history, and films based on the racial roots of gun control. Jews for the Preservation of Firearms seeks to end gun control and to educate the Jewish community about the atrocities that Jews suffered while unarmed. Their website provides articles, information on the Bill of Rights, and networking for members of JPFO.

Law Enforcement Alliance of America (LEAA)

7700 Leesburg Pike Suite 421, Falls Church, VA   22043
phone: (703) 847-2677
website: www.leaa.org

The Law Enforcement Alliance of America is a coalition of law enforcement personnel, crime victims, and citizens who seek to reduce instances of violent crime in the United States while promoting the rights of individuals to defend themselves. The Law Enforcement Alliance is the largest non-profit, non-partisan organization of its kind, and, provides access to publications about current events concerning gun legislation, gun rights, and true accounts of self-defense on the LEAA website.

National Rifle Association of America (NRA)
11250 Waples Mill Road, Fairfax, VA 22030
phone: (800) 392-3867
website: www.nra.org

Since its inception in 1871, the National Rifle Association of America has become one of the nation's foremost promoters of gun rights, shooting sports, and firearm safety and education programs. Though it began as an organization to train soldiers to shoot rifles in a scientifically-calculated manner, over the past 139 years, the NRA has morphed into a major political force, and the largest provider of firearms education in the world. The NRA's website provides comprehensive information about current gun rights issues, guns and hunting, updates on legislative action, NRA program materials, and publications.

Second Amendment Foundation (SAF)
12500 N.E. 10th Place, Bellevue, WA 98005
phone: (206) 454-7012
website: www.saf.org

The Second Amendment Foundation seeks to inform the general public about the history of firearms possession, and through legal action and educational programs, inform the public about the issues surrounding the gun control debate. The Second Amendment Foundation provides extensive information on gun rights and laws, as well as contact information for reaching legislators on the SAF website.

Shooter's Committee on Political Education (SCOPE)
PO Box 12711, Rochester, NY 14612
phone: (585) 663-8741
website: www.scopeny.org

Founded in 1965, the Shooter's Committee on Political Education is New York's leading Second Amendment Civil Rights Organization. The mission of the Shooter's Committee on Political Education is to inform members about current gun legislation, stop gun control legislation in the state of New York, and to educate the public about firearm ownership and their Second Amendment rights. SCOPE's website provides newsletters and legislative updates of interest to gun rights advocates.

Students for Concealed Carry on Campus (SCCC)

e-mail: organizers@concealedcampus.org
website: www.concealedcampus.org

Students for Concealed Carry on Campus is a national organization of school employees, students, parents, and concerned citizens who promote the lawful carry of concealed weapons on college campuses. Students for Concealed Carry on Campus believes that concealed weapons permit holders should have the same rights to carry their weapons on campus as they do off campus, and believe that instances of multiple murders are more likely in gun-free zones such as college campuses. The SCCC's website gives crime statistics, state laws, arguments for concealed carry on college campuses, and information on volunteering.

Students for Gun Free Schools (SGFS)

Newcomb Hall, Charlottesville, VA   22903
fax: (703) 631-8997
e-mail: info@studentsforgunfreeschools.org
website: www.studentsforgunfreeschools.org

Students for Gun Free Schools is an organization founded to honor one of the victims of the April 2007 Virginia Tech shootings. Students for Gun Free Schools promotes gun control on college campuses and believes that concealed weapons on campuses endanger other students and detract from a healthy learning environment. Students for Gun Free Schools opposes attempts to force colleges and universities to allow concealed weapons carriers to bring their firearms onto college campuses. News and volunteer information are available on SGFS's website.

Violence Policy Center (VPC)
1730 Rhode Island Avenue NW Suite 1014
Washington, DC   20036
phone: (202) 822 8200
website: www.vpc.org

The Violence Policy Center based in Washington, DC is a non-profit organization leading the fight against gun violence through education, political action, and policy advocacy. The Violence Policy Center views gun violence as a public health issue, and believes that firearms should be required to meet health and safety standards. The VPC website provides access to publication, press releases, and articles on assault weapons, gun violence, gun lobbies, and the gun industry.

Bibliography

Books

Massad Ayoob   *The Gun Digest Book of Concealed Carry.* Iola, WI: Gun Digest Books, 2008.

Brian Doherty   *Gun Control on Trial: Inside the Supreme Court Battle over the Second Amendment.* Washington, DC: Cato Institute, 2008.

Kristin A. Goss   *Disarmed: The Missing Movement for Gun Control in America.* Princeton, NJ: Princeton University Press, 2006.

Adam Gottlieb   *America Fights Back: Armed
and Dave   Self-Defense in a Violent Age.*
Workman   Kenmore, NY: Merril Press, October 30, 2007.

William T.   *Showdown in the Show-Me State: The
Horner   Fight over Conceal-and-Carry Gun Laws in Missouri.* Columbia, MO: University of Missouri Press, June 2005.

John Longenecker   *Safe Streets in the Nationwide Concealed Carry of Handguns—Meeting Dependency and Violent Crime with American Spirit, Independence, and Citizen Authority.* Los Angeles, CA: Contrast Media Press, June 7, 2008.

John Longenecker *Transfer of Wealth: The Case For Nationwide Concealed Carry of Handguns.* Los Angeles, CA: Contrast Media Press, December 2, 2005.

John R. Lott, Jr. *More Guns, Less Crime: Understanding Crime and Gun Control Laws.* Chicago, IL: University of Chicago Press, May 24, 2010.

Howard Nemerov *Four Hundred Years of Gun Control . . . Why Isn't it Working?* Los Angeles, CA: Contrast Media Press, May 5, 2008.

Brian Anse Patrick *Rise of the Anti-Media: In-Forming America's Concealed Weapon Carry Movement.* Lanham, MD: Lexington Books, December 31, 2009.

Mark Pogrebin, N. Prabha Unnithan, and Paul Stretesky *Guns, Violence, and Criminal Behavior: The Offender's Perspective.* Boulder, CO: Lynne Rienner Publishers, September 30, 2009.

Robert J. Spitzer *The Politics of Gun Control.* Washington, DC: CQ Press, July 16, 2007.

Mark Walters and Kathy Jackson *Lessons from Armed America.* Hamilton, MI: White Feather Press, September 24, 2009.

Harry L. Wilson *Guns, Gun Control, and Elections.* Lanham, MD: Rowman and Littlefield Publishers, 2007.

Michael E. Wuest   *The Great American Gun Control Debate (Not)!* Bloomington, IN: Author House, 2010.

Periodicals

Alex Altman   "The Future of Gun Control," *Time*, June 26, 2008.

Christopher Barron   "Concealed Carry: If You're Interested in Preventing Hate Crimes, Let's Stop Them Before They Happen," *The Huffington Post*, June 10, 2009.

Steve Chapman   "Chicago's Misfire on Gun Violence," *Human Events*, April 24, 2008.

Gail Collins   "Have Gun, Will Travel," *New York Times*, July 31, 2009.

Bill Confer   "Right to Self-Defense Should Know No Borders," *New American*, July 27, 2009.

Ann Coulter   "Let's Make America a Sad-Free Zone!" *Human Events*, April 17, 2007.

Richard A. Epstein   "Court Wrong on the Chicago Gun Case," *Forbes*, July 6, 2010.

Adam Freedman   "Clause and Effect," *New York Times*, December 16, 2007.

Bob Herbert   "A Culture Soaked in Blood," *New York Times*, April 24, 2009.

Robert A. Levy   "They Never Learn," *The American Spectator*, April 25, 2007.

Megan McArdle   "The Power of the Gun," *The Atlantic*, August 27, 2009.

Stephanie Mencimer   "Whitewashing the Second Amendment," *Mother Jones*, March 20, 2008.

Erich Pratt   "When Will Unarmed Victims Get their Apology from Uncle Sam?" *Gun Owners of America*, July 6, 2010.

David Rittgers   "Be a Good Victim," *National Review*, October 22, 2009.

Suzanne Smalley   "More Guns on Campus?" *Newsweek*, February 15, 2008.

Thomas Sowell   "Gun-Control Laws," *National Review*, Jun 29, 2010.

Andrew Sullivan   "More Guns = More or Less Crime?" *The Atlantic*, April 17, 2007.

Robert Verbruggen   "Gun Rights are Civil Rights," *National Review*, July 7, 2010.

Robert Verbruggen   "More Handguns, Less Crime—or More?" *The American Spectator*, June 21, 2010.

Kelley Beaucar Vlahos   "Will the Obama Administration Come for Your Guns?" *The American Conservative*, May 18, 2009.

Index